Letters

A British-Born American Returns to the Mean Streets of His Youth to Share His Life Changed by Faith

May God bless this book to your heart, Helen.
Frank

By Frank J. Rossiter

Letters from Liverpool

This title is also available as an eBook.
Visit www.CreativeForcePress.com/titles for more information.

Published by Creative Force Press
4704 Pacific Ave, Suite C, Lacey, WA 98503
www.CreativeForcePress.com

ISBN: 978-1-939989-02-4

Printed in the United States of America

Dedication

I dedicate this story with love to my Best Friend,
Lord and Savior, Jesus Christ.

"*For God so loved the world, that He gave His only begotten Son, that whosoever believes on Him shall not perish, but have everlasting life.*"

John 3:16

Table of Contents

Foreword

I want to take you, the reader, on a journey; a journey that I hope leaves you reflective of your own journey through life. It's a good story, not because I'm writing it, but because of the One who inspired it. To get the full impact of what you're about to read, it would be beneficial for you to have read my book, *Frankie Boy,* about my life growing up in the inner city of Liverpool following World War II. I was 24 years of age at the end of that book, and now I am 73 (I swear I don't look a day over 72). Ouch! That's a lot of years unaccounted for in between!

If I'd gone on to live a normal life after "*Frankie Boy,*" there would be no need for a sequel. But it has been anything but normal, as you will see. And I promise not to paint a pretty picture of myself; for in me you will see all the frailties of the human heart exposed, just as I tried to do in *Frankie Boy.* I am ordinary beyond belief. Remember this as you read *Letters from Liverpool.* It's a testimony of God's love and grace in spite of me. But first, let me share my story of how I became a Christian, so you'll have a good understanding of where I've come from. I wrote this testimony to hand out to my tennis buddies, because of their constant digs about my religious faith.

That's me - the third one from the left.

"The Boys of Summer"

My Testimony

I want to talk a little about Christianity. Now, I understand that most people would rather sit in a dentist chair than sit in a church and listen to preaching about hellfire and brimstone. I get that. But I guarantee you this will be painless, and nothing like you've heard before. Whether you read on, or quit right here, makes no difference to me. I'm going ahead anyway.

About a month ago, in a YouTube debate, I listened carefully to the intellectual, Christopher Hitchens, as he stated his reasons for not believing in God. Last night I heard the same thing from Bill Maher, except he berated and ridiculed a lot more. Instead of reacting to them, I found myself admiring both men for their honesty. It wasn't their intention to hurt or shock people; they believed in what they were saying, which I found refreshing. Below is an excerpt:

"None of us have ever seen God. No one can prove that there is a God. No one can prove that the Bible is true. So, in human reasoning or common sense terms, religious people could just be fooling themselves. It is comforting to believe that their misdeeds are forgiven and they're going to a beautiful place called Heaven after they die."

I was a skeptic once, so I understand why they think like that. I don't blame them. All I can do now is tell you why I believe. The rest is up to you. I do it not to win you over, but to give you something to think about other than what you hear the "Hitchen's" and "Maher's" of the world saying.

I was born in Liverpool, England, and raised Catholic. Being Catholic was fine. I didn't think much about it one way or the other. As a young boy, I didn't like going to church or confession. When I was old enough to make my own decisions, I pretty much left it all behind. It wasn't so much a rejection as it was just a plain disinterest.

Fast forward and I'm now about thirty years old, living in Olympia, Washington, with a wife and four children. They go to church (not Catholic) every Sunday while I stay in bed. I have no interest whatsoever. Yet, somehow, my beautiful wife manages to talk me into going just this once. It's her birthday. All my excuses aren't sufficient to overcome her desire for me to go. I take my last drag on a Camel cigarette and enter the church. Two hours later, I stumble outside and light up another Camel and inhale deeply. I am in trouble; confused; bewildered. I look into my wife's face, curling my lips into the nastiest snarl I can muster. "Don't ever ask me to go in there again." She is shocked and hurt by my angry countenance. Her sad face turns away. I watch her walk the four children to the car to wait while I finish my cigarette.

I have no idea why I reacted like that. I can only say that I was affected in some strange way by what I had heard. Some Christians would say that was "God dealing with me, wanting me to get right with Him." At that time, I would've called that crazy talk. The following Sunday morning, my wife quietly goes about getting the kids ready for church, and is mildly surprised to see me getting ready to go too. She had no idea why, and neither did I. It was just one of those unexplainable moments in time.

Half-way through the service I began to tremble. By the end of the service I was a bit of a basket case again. But this time, for some strange reason, I didn't want to leave. I felt my wife's hand in mine as she whispered, "I'll go with you." I took a deep breath thinking, this is so out of character for me. Nevertheless, I stood and let myself be led down the aisle to the altar at the front. The four kids followed behind. I talked to God the only way I knew how. I said, "If this is real, then I want what you have for me." I couldn't bear the thought that it might be phony. I had no idea how God was going to prove it to me, or if He even wanted to.

The first indication that life wasn't going to be quite the same was when I discovered a real hunger for reading the Bible. At the time, my wife was using a New Testament called "Good News for Modern Man." What's more amazing is that I understood everything I was reading. Within weeks I quit the band I had formed a couple of years earlier. Then I sold my amp, guitar, sound system, records, and the lot. I was now branded a religious fanatic by all my friends and co-workers. The very thing I'd feared the most had come upon me. I couldn't stop talking about Jesus.

If you non-believers quit reading now, I would understand. But, if you're just a little bit curious, read on. Just remember, I'm not responsible for what happens to you if you do continue.

Okay, being honest, I'm now really into this thing...Big Time. Church Sunday morning and evening, and Bible study every Wednesday. I opened up my little family restaurant in town in the evenings in order to minister to people off the street and talk to them about Jesus. If you knew me, you would know that all of this is absolutely not my M.O. Maybe, just maybe, I've flipped out, or something or somebody is in the process of changing me. That should be kind of scary, but, I found I was rather enjoying the change. Now, I should avoid talking about this next area because it's so controversial, even in some Christian circles, but I'm going to anyway. So, you, the reader, can drop out any time you think you've heard enough.

The Bible talks a lot about the believer being filled with the Holy Spirit who gives you the power to live the Christian life. One of the manifestations of being filled is you begin to speak in an unknown or heavenly language. Now, if people think you're over the top already, this ain't gonna help dispel that notion at all. It only adds to the notion that you've now slipped into the twilight zone, for sure.

No matter. If it would help me be a better Christian, then I wanted it. I needed all the help I could get. So I asked God for it. And asked, and asked...nothing. I gave up asking. Then one day I decided to ask again. After all, wasn't it in God's best interest to give me something that would help me be a better Christian?

I knelt at the altar. A voice or a thought came into my head telling me to go into the prayer room. I got up without questioning and walked into the quietness of the prayer room. My knees no sooner hit the bench when this warmth began to wash over me; starting from my head on down, filling up my stomach, then rising to come out of my mouth. My hands went up in praise as I listened with amazement and joy, at this language bubbling or babbling out of me. I don't know how long I was there. I was oblivious to time and my surroundings. When I did walk out of the prayer room, my wife stood waiting for me. One look at me and she smiled.

"It happened, didn't it?" All I could do was nod, yes.

The Dream

It wasn't long after this when I had a dream. It confused me a little because I felt that I was already awake with my eyes open. It felt strange peering into the darkness of the bedroom, like I'd been watching something on a screen and the screen went blank. The dream (or vision) was about my family back in Liverpool, England; my brother Joe, in particular.

There were creatures like sea horses sailing in the sky, with people sitting on them, much like you would see on a merry-go-round. It was fun and everybody on them was laughing and having a good time. My eyes were drawn to the one carrying my brother, Joe, and his wife (then girlfriend) who sat behind him. Joe was having such a good time he was unaware that the sea creature had flipped his girlfriend off its back. I watched in horror as she tumbled down, falling through the air headed for her demise.

The dream vision ended before she hit the ground. Thank goodness for that! We're all used to waking up from nasty dreams and breathing a sigh of relief. What made this one different was my certainty that I was already awake, laying there watching it unfold...

Do Christians Have Vivid Imaginations?

And do they think God is showing them things or speaking to them in order to get them to do certain things? Well, though the Bible is full of stories about Him doing just that, we mortals always doubt He would do that to us. First, I had to define what I thought the dream was about. My wife and I felt God was showing me the lost state of my family in Liverpool, and to prepare to go and share the Gospel (Good News) with them. In reality, that would be a tall order indeed. We had four small children and were barely surviving from paycheck to paycheck. Still, I threw out the challenge to God.

"If you provide the means, we will go."

It remained there in the back of my mind. I never dwelt on it or was overly obsessed about it. In time, it began to fade.

The Coffee Shop

A few months later, I was walking through town with a friend when I suddenly stopped and peered into the window of a small 'mom and pop' coffee shop.

"I got this strange feeling God wants me to buy this place."

My friend looked a little surprised, to say the least.

"I don't see any for sale sign, Frank."

I walked inside anyway. The place was empty except for a man I assumed was the owner. He looked up.

"I think I'm supposed to buy this place." I'm smiling because it felt like I was playing a silly game of sorts. I had absolutely no money to offer him. He looked just as surprised as did my friend a few minutes before.

"How could you have known I was just thinking about the possibility of selling it?" he responded.

"I don't have any money," I confessed. Maybe now this game would end right here, I thought. He took a long look at me before speaking.

"That's okay. Maybe we can work something out."

And that's how I found myself the proud, but very scared, owner of my first **coffee shop**. I named it **"HIS PLACE,"** meaning God's place. We piped in Christian music and put in a rack with Christian books for sale and for people to borrow. That should have scared off all but the devoted followers of Jesus, right? Wrong. They came anyway, lining up for a variety of delicious homemade soups and specials I had perfected over a dozen years working in restaurants.

New Direction

Things were going along fine until about a year into our adventure. One night about closing time, I'm behind the counter cleaning things up when, out of the blue, I get the thought, "sell the restaurant and use the proceeds to purchase tickets to go to Liverpool." It is so hard for me to say I heard a voice, when it could just as easily have been a thought that had crossed my mind. I was still pondering the 'thought' when my wife came back from running errands.

I said, "Guess what?" She stopped in mid-stride and looked at me.

"I know. He told me the same thing as I was coming around the corner."

Now I'm getting really freaked out. "He told you what?"

"To sell the restaurant and use the money for England." She turned and walked back toward the door.

"Now where are you going?"

"To make plane reservations for six." She was out the door before I could muster a protest. Her faith had always been much stronger than mine. Even after all that had transpired, I still questioned whether God could possibly be interested in such small potatoes, when He had the whole universe to worry about. On top of it all, we decided not to advertise or put a for-sale sign in the window. This would be the ultimate test whether God was in this or we had created the whole thing out of our own imaginings.

When it got closer to the time the tickets were to be paid (seven days before departure), our faith began to wane. This drove us to our knees behind the counter. Members of our church family would come by, always asking the inevitable question. "Any bites on the business yet?" The answer was always the same. "No, not yet, but we know he's on the way."

A Buyer!

Reader, hang on to your seat. You will find the next part hard to believe, and who would blame you. The day before the tickets were to be paid for, a small unassuming older man walks in and stands there looking the place over. I asked if I could help him. He said he was looking for a little business to purchase. Something he could handle himself and keep him busy in his retirement. I was speechless. The one and only prospect we had was standing there in front of me. I told him it was indeed for sale. He confessed he didn't know anything about running a restaurant. If we would consider working with him for a week, he would not only buy it now, he would let us keep all the week's proceeds.

There will always be those who, no matter what, will scoff at any idea of a God working in the affairs of men. No amount of proof will ever convince them. I'm not saying the above story is convincing in itself. Although it was happening to me, I still found it incredible to think that God could ever be that personally involved in my life. But the story isn't over yet, so hang on.

During that last week, we sold off all our earthly possessions – all except our almost new washer and dryer. No one showed an interest in them. We would have no choice but to leave them there. On the day of our departure, we cleaned the floor and backed out the door of our rented house, so as not to leave any footprints. As we turned around, a young couple drove up and came around to meet us.

"Are we too late for the sale?"

"All we have left is the washer and dryer set. They're just like new," I said. "That's exactly what we came for!" They wrote a check, loaded them up and drove away!

Faith-Building

A lot of coincidences? Maybe. But why, if it was God, does He always seem to make you wait until the last minute to answer? My short answer to that is, "the testing of your faith." Faith is believing without seeing. It takes faith to believe in God, and faith, like a muscle, has to be tested and strengthened.

When I first became a Christian, I went forward to receive a promise. That was my faith in action. I could have very easily walked out and that would have been the end of it. So God sees my faith and tests it. He tests it again and again. My faith holds. Then, and only then, do I begin to see and experience God working in my life. **Faith is the key that unlocks the mystery of God...**You may say, "I don't believe in God because..." and come up with a thousand reasons why you don't believe and they would all be good-sounding reasons. But what if I said to you, "Do you really want to know? If you really want to, you can know for sure." What would your reaction be then? That gets pretty scary, doesn't it? Because you know as well as I do that, if God does reveal Himself to you, life can never be the same again. And that's true. You will be changed forever, just like I was. All your legitimate reasons to say, "I don't believe" will become illegitimate. You will now be required to act upon that which you now know to be true. You may lose all your friends because you know they will probably laugh at you for "getting religion."

Back to My Story

My wife and I, along with four children ranging in age from nine to thirteen, arrive on the doorstep of my not-so-happy step dad's house in Liverpool. Squeezing another six bodies into an already full house was a very difficult experience indeed, but somehow we managed. One of our first visitors was my brother, Joe. Remember him from my dream vision? We sat at the kitchen table where he revealed to me how excited he was when he heard we were coming over to England. When I told him about the dream, he "accepted Jesus into his heart" right then and there. His girlfriend accepted Jesus not long after.

My Family

Finding a Church

Shortly after we arrived, my wife and I were out for a walk when our attention was drawn to a banner across the front of a church that read, **JESUS IS ALIVE!**

On Sunday, we took our kids and sat in the back row. After the service, the pastor came off the podium and walked right up to where we were sitting and asked us to come in to his office.

Finding a Home

There, he told us that he had been praying for the Lord to send a family that could occupy and fix up the Falkner Street house. It would be used for housing foreign Christian students attending the nearby university. By now, we were used to seeing God work in mysterious ways. What He forgot to tell us was the atrocious condition the house was in!

On the outside, it looked like an old, three-story house set in a quiet, and what used to be, upscale neighborhood. Wow, God, what a reward for being good. Then the pastor opened the massive front door. Our little family followed him inside. Gasp! This once lovely spacious home, with wide staircase and lofty, sculptured ceilings, was totally destroyed. Wiring and light fixtures dangled from gaping holes in the ceilings. Doors and windows were smashed. Ugly graffiti had been sprayed all over the walls. Wallpaper lay shredded and strewn over the bare floorboards along with human feces. Broken glass crunched beneath us with every step. We opened the bathroom door, startling a hoard of pigeons that escaped through a huge hole in the ceiling. We navigated up the stairs badly scarred with motorcycle tracks.

We chose the cavernous front room, the least damaged one, to settle in. Word got out, and soon the house was bustling with activity as willing hands washed, painted, and wallpapered to some semblance of its former glory. There was enough donated food to feed the volunteers, and our family, when the day's work was done.

Divine Provision

It was a very exciting time in our lives to see God meet all of our needs. But still, He kept us on the edge. That thing called faith had to keep being tested.

My older sister Leslie, who had also received Jesus into her heart, came to me with her concern. "Frankie, your children need shoes. Don't be too proud now. That's what the 'Sosh' (Social Services) is there for." I told her that God would provide, and promptly forgot about it. A week later she approached me again. I felt I was being a poor example to her by neglecting my family's needs. I relented and went down to the welfare office and was given enough money for shoes and clothing for the kids. When I got home, there was a letter from America in the letter box. I rushed upstairs to put the kettle on. We had a 'nice cuppa tea' while opening our treasure. Getting mail from home was always one of the highlights of our time there, especially because it took ten to fourteen days to get there. When I opened it, I almost fell off my chair. I held in my hand a check for the same amount of money I had just received. The letter said in part:

"Dear Frank, while praying at our Christian Businessmen's meeting, I sensed the Lord prompting me to take up a collection for you. When I told the group, one other person said he received the same message."

I couldn't wait to share the story with the Christians working on the house, and especially with Joe and Leslie. I wanted them to see God's faithfulness so their faith would also grow. Then I shocked everybody by announcing that I was going to give the money back to the 'Sosh.' My brother wanted to go with me (I don't think he believed I would actually do it). The timing could not have been more dramatic. It was closing time on Christmas Eve weekend. When we arrived at the welfare office, there was a crowd of angry people gathered around the front entrance. They were struggling to keep the door open. On the inside was a doorman in a tug-of-war trying to pull it shut. I managed to get close enough to shout through the opening, "I don't want anything. I just want to bring money back!"

Well, now…there was no way he was gonna fall for that little trick and, with a scowl, finally yanked the door shut. A woman next to me, holding a baby, began to cry. I turned to her and took hold of her hand. I put the money in it as I told her, "Jesus loves you. Merry Christmas." As I walked away my heart was bursting with joy. My brother and I walked back to the house in silence.

It was the most profound thing I had ever done.

I am writing this story forty years after the fact. I may not have convinced even one skeptic to take a step toward God. But now that you have read this far, at the very least, you are a little wiser as to what makes a Christian so sure about something so intangible. In all my life of being a Christian, I have never once doubted the existence of God, nor the unconditional love that He has for me. Even at 73 and happily retired in Arizona, I am ready to go at a moment's notice, anywhere He chooses to send me. I have a feeling He may take me up on that someday.

If you search for God with your intellect, as do people like

Christopher Hitchins and Bill Maher, you will always come up empty-handed. You will never find Him. But God does promise that if you search for Him with all your *heart*, He will be found of you.

To know the One who created all things out of nothing, you must first clothe yourself with a little humility, something very hard to find in wise and learned men.

As you can see, I tried not to get too preachy or hit you with a bunch of Bible verses. If you don't think God even exists, throwing Bible verses at you is not going to convince you that He does. But when you hear first-hand about a life like mine that has been changed, then maybe God can nudge you to take the first step toward Him.

That is really what it's all about. After that, the Bible will come alive and the Spirit of God will take you on a journey of discovery that never ends, and will never cease to amaze you!

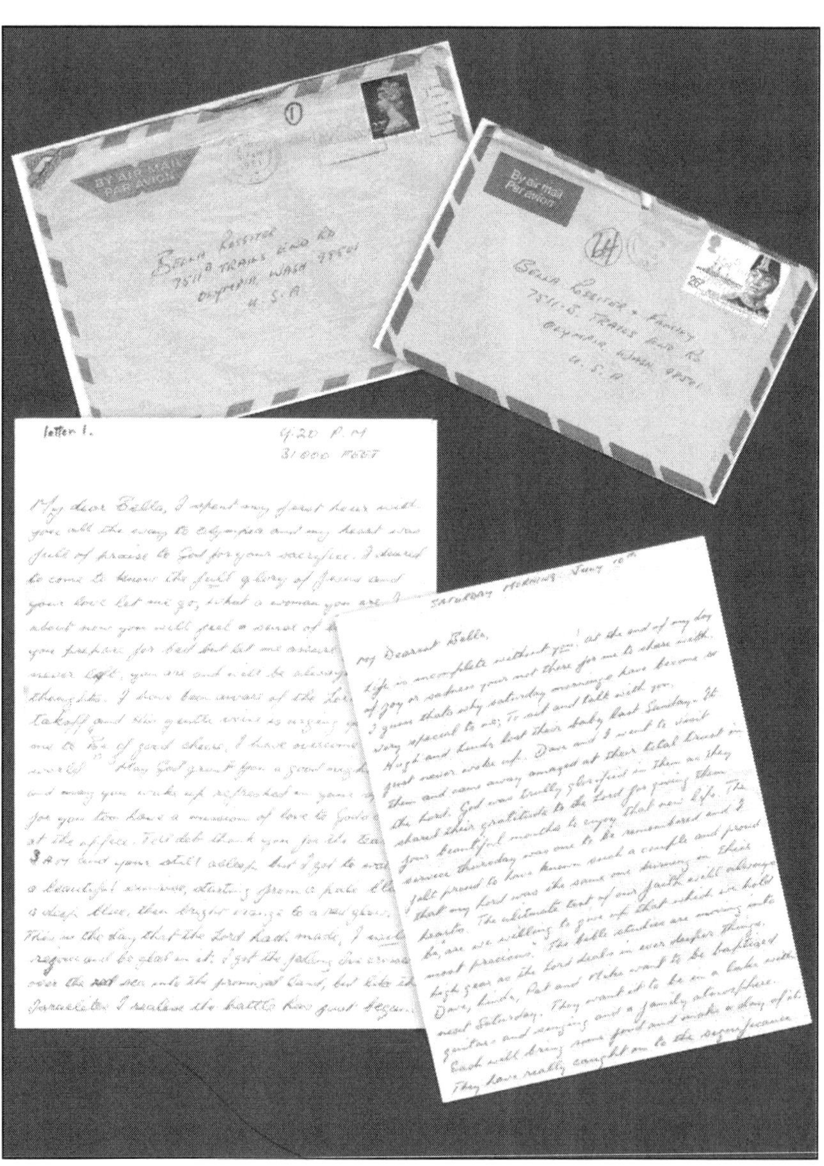
BY AIR MAIL
PAR AVION
By air mail
Par avion
U.S.A.
letter 1.
4:20 P.M
31000 FEET
My dear Bella,
SATURDAY MORNING
My Dearest Bella,

PART I

Bye Dad…

1981

February 2nd

My dear Bella,

I spent my first hour with you all the way to the airport and my heart was full of praise to God for your sacrifice. I desired to come to know the full glory of Jesus and your love let me go. What a woman you are. Just about now, you will feel a sense of loneliness as you prepare for bed, but let me assure you, I have never left. You are and will always be in my thoughts. I have been aware of the Lord since takeoff and His gentle voice is urging you and me to *"Be of good cheer, I have overcome the world."* May God grant you a good night's sleep and may you wake up refreshed in your spirit, for you, too, have a mission of love to God's children at the office.

3:00 a.m. and you're still asleep but I got to watch a beautiful sunrise, starting from a pale blue to a deep blue, then bright orange to a red glow. *"This is the day the Lord hath made, I will rejoice and be glad in it."* I got the feeling I've crossed over the Red Sea into the Promised Land, but like the Israelites, I realize the battle has just begun. But, *"the battle is mine, saith the Lord."* So I commit it all into His hands. I prayed for you all while you were sleeping and laid my hand on each head. Two more hours till London, but it's been a good trip so far. I prayed for all on board that they may come to know the love of God.

And so it was that I came into the land of my birth. I had left behind a wife and four children, ages twenty, nineteen, eighteen and sixteen, for what I consider now in my old age, a foolish adventure indeed. I was not a missionary in the classic sense; nor a Bible scholar, nor did I spend a lot of time on my knees in fasting and prayer. In other words, I was going without much equipment, up there in my brain or down there in my heart. Maybe it was true that part of me was running away from my responsibilities as a father and a husband. Nevertheless, I was on my way and thought I was ready for this boldness to be tested in the fire of reality.

NOTE: *Though I did write and receive letters from my sons, Tony, Frank Jr, and Jim, I consider them too personal to share and will just concentrate on my correspondence to my wife.*

Sunday, February 7th

I spent a good hour at the hospital, singing and praying softly to Nin (my grandmother) but there was no indication that she was aware of me. I gently stroked her hair and asked her over and over if she understood that I loved her. Finally, her eyes opened for a split second and I knew she had used all her power to let me know she had heard. I held her hand and wept for her and she gave my hand the slightest squeeze. That was yesterday. Today all the family is there; it's just a matter of time now. But, my God is waiting there too, to take her home to be with Him. Isn't that what life is all about? He is our hope for all the tomorrows. How can the world ignore so great a salvation? When life is over, I'm going home.

Well, Bella. I haven't found work yet, but I've never felt stronger in spirit. England is in a very bad way, with thousands out of work daily. It's like an epidemic of doom settling over the whole country. But, my God is standing by to "*heal the brokenhearted, to preach deliverance to the captives, to set at liberty them that are bruised.*" This people have ignored God for too long and this is the only way He can get their attention, because He loves them.

Wednesday 1:30 a.m.

God, how these people need the Lord. Everywhere I go I hear such unashamed profanity and abusive lifestyles. It is like God poured out one of those vials in Revelation, and they are cursing Him. But He has given me a love for them and I look forward to some fruit, no matter how small. Just one life snatched from Hell would make it all worthwhile. Pray that God would break me into a million pieces so I can't ever be me again. My family here were sure you and I broke up when I came back home to live. Lord, if they only knew the love you and I share. God's ways are past finding out.

2 a.m.

I am all moved in at Susan's and my room looks great. You would be very proud of me. It is bright and cheerful like a picture out of a magazine. I'm inspired to do the whole house like my room. My brother Tommy just brought up a couple of English hamburgers and a cup of tea that he made just for me. He has responded to me very well and I feel sure he likes having me around.

Meanwhile, everything is going so beautifully, so don't you worry, not even for a second, for I sense a great peace about everything I do, like the Lord has finally been able to take over and I walk without fear. I have never felt quite like this before. Everywhere I go I am aware of myself bringing peace and joy and a sense of order, and it's marvelous to see. I seem to be powerless to do otherwise. Praise God, why didn't I give in sooner, old blockhead me. (*Nin died soon after this letter.*)

Thursday Evening

Talked to a lady by the name of Sarah today, Bella. She's middle aged and finds herself pregnant and she just can't handle another baby. Very distraught lady. She wants to have an abortion. Keep Sarah in your prayers.

I thought it would interest you to know half the country wishes someone would assassinate Margaret Thatcher and the other half is holding their breath hoping the country won't go under completely. She will not budge one inch as business after business folds up, throwing thousands out of work every day. Her policy is, *"If you're not competitive with the world market, you deserve to go out of business. There will be no more government handouts."* Well, England's whole economy is built on the fact that if business is losing money, government will step in to save all those jobs and that isn't true anymore. She is letting them go right to the bottom so that workers will know she is dead serious. They will have to work harder, for their very livelihood is at stake. There are no free handouts for the *"dolers"*, either. Now they have to do community work equivalent to their dole. I'm loving every minute of it; but I dare not let anybody know that. Hope old Margaret can hold out to the end. We might get a little pride back in this country.

The weather has turned ice cold with snow all day today. You'll never believe what I wore to go to Pastor Rowland's church. Undies, two pair of socks, thermals, tracksuit, shirt, jeans, pullover, coat, hat and gloves. Needless to say I couldn't raise my hands to praise or anything, so I just sat like a big stuffed teddy bear. I'm in bed with most of it still on. Ha!

No job yet but I stay busy. I have no needs and I am always helpful, so it's easy to have me around. I have not had one bad day, and I bring peace and a smile to all I meet. That is why I know the Lord is with me. I walk one day at a time and desire to see no further, for He alone knows the way, so I may as well let Him lead me.

Saturday Morning, February 28th

I can see why I love you so much and can see why I trust Him to be there when you need Him. I am at peace because He is faithful in caring for my precious family. Praise His wonderful Holy name! When I look around I sometimes wonder if He died in vain, then I think of you and me and a host of the faithful that I know and I say, "Thank God you came, Jesus, for where would we be if you hadn't?" What despair if we had no Lord, no hope, no faith in a better way. What and who else can offer us love, joy, peace in such a troubled world as this. If He had given us a paradise, we would have no need for Him. Thank you Lord for such a world as this, for in it I came to realize my need for you.

Met up with Sarah again. She was adamant about going ahead with the abortion. I could see there was nothing I could say or do to change the situation. She was totally incapable of accepting another pregnancy. While she was waiting for a call back from a doctor, I went for a walk and talked to the Lord about it. By the time I got back, I had His answer and she was going to hear it, whether she liked it or not. I picked up the Bible and she knew what was coming. I showed her in *I Corinthians 12* how God, by His Spirit, gives gifts to all believers, and while on my walk, He gave me the gift of wisdom to tell you how He feels about the whole thing.

"At the moment of conception it is a living soul, given life by Him and He alone can take back that life. He will take full responsibility for the life He has given and for you to trust that He will not put any more on you than you can bear. You have said you trusted Him for salvation, but the fruit of that trust will be in trusting that His hand is on the baby." She was silent for a long time, then she said, complaining, *"If I change my mind, everybody will know it was because you talked me out of it."*

I said, *"Sarah, I could see there was nobody on earth that could have talked you out of it. So I didn't even try, even though I would gladly give my life for it. But when God talks, I think we had better listen."* I left it all in the Lord's hands and came home.

The weather here is real nasty with wind and gusty rain most of the time. I bundle up pretty good but I get to feeling sorry for the older people when I see them outside waiting for a bus or doing their daily shopping (most people shop for every meal because they don't have refrigerators). Sometimes I just go for a walk and give a smile to each passing face, bringing a ray of warmth to a cold heart. But most of the time I'm inside decorating, reading or playing with Susan's kids. I go visiting but not a lot and try to make it short and sweet. Most come to Susan's and see me there and gaze on my masterpiece of homemaking. Just finished the bathroom late last night and it looked so good I took a bath at 1 a.m.

The sum of my whole experience in Liverpool is peace. Knowing God is working to bring me to a place of rest and trust in Him so the world won't ever again be my temptation. I will be His forever. And you, Bella, have made it all possible so you will get to share the fruit of your sacrifice.

Thursday, March 5th

Had a strange week to say the least, but a fulfilling one. I smile as I reflect on the ways of the Lord. Guess it all started last Sunday when I got this feeling I would like to wear Mr. Little's sandwich board for a day. That sure wasn't like me, but come Monday the feeling was still with me so I headed for town to seek out my little friend. But, alas! He was nowhere to be found. I became a bit put out and walked all over town in search of him, ending up outside Woolworth's where he usually stands.

By now I was frantic. So obsessed was I to carry that thing that I felt like crying as I headed for the Pier Head where he sometimes hangs out. The banner now became His cross and in my mind I could see Jesus fall under the weight of it as the crowds watched on each side of the street. Some, I felt, wanted to help Him but were afraid of what the rest would think. I found myself praying, Lord, I will, if you would help me find Mr. Little. I was totally captivated with the thought that I would be proud to walk among the crowds, a fool for such a wonderful one as Jesus.

How unreal the whole thing seemed to me, yet I enjoyed the feeling of closeness I felt with the Lord of Glory. I never did find Mr. Little that day, but I knew I would be back again. The next morning, Tuesday, I stood waiting for a bus to town when I spotted this poor old guy pushing a hand cart with a load of scrap iron, when my eyes were drawn to his hands. They were blue from the icy wind and I felt a little ashamed, me all bundled up with my leather gloves on. Just about then, the bus pulled up and I hesitated, as I remembered my words to the Moen's that very morning as I wrote, *I want to be Jesus' hands reaching out to those in need,* and I found myself running across the road. The old man stared in wide-eyed disbelief as I told him, *Here, put these on.* In a weak voice he said, *"But, won't your hands be cold now?" No, not any more.* As I touched his cold hand I said, "*I did that for Jesus.*" Standing at the bus stop, I watched as he fumbled to put the gloves on, then his face looked across the street at me and somehow I knew how he felt. Warm inside, like I was feeling. Bella, I felt so good, I was looking for someone I could give my jacket to!

Mr. Little hesitated for the longest time when I finally caught up with him and told him I wanted to carry his banner. Only after I assured him it was the Lord's idea, did he promise to bring me one the next day. So, I did something I thought I could never do. I walked through the heart of Liverpool, proclaiming Jesus as Lord. Talk about the joy of the Lord! My feet never touched ground once, I was in heaven the whole time. I had a smile as big as the sandwich board I was carrying and loved every minute of it. I was led to talk to a young guy who had an outdoor girly magazine stall, and in ten minutes we became good friends. He is now reading my book. Walking through St. John's Market, I passed by two guys working a meat stall. One of them looked up and tried to read all the sign board before I passed by, so I stopped till he finished. He let his friend serve while we had a good chat and he, too, wanted to read my book.

I met many interesting people and I even went home on the bus with the sign still on me. I felt so good I didn't want to take it off. Well, today I did it again, but this time it was a little harder going. I was more aware of how people were seeing me and my hands were clammy. I had butterflies too, and found myself praying more out of my need. I asked myself if I was meant to do it only the once, and I was out of God's will today. But, God in his love showed me that I was more of a sacrifice to Him today than I was yesterday. So I came to realize His strength in my weakness was what I longed for most. I stood a little taller and I smiled a little more and I told those passing faces, *"No, it is not easy for me, but I'm doing it for Jesus."* If He is pleased with me, then all is well. I may even go back tomorrow.

Friday 5 p.m.

Got up late today, Bella, and I felt like maybe I shouldn't go to town. But within a half hour, I was down there with my sign board on and had a great time. Carl, at the magazine stall, had only read half my book, but his partner had read it all and liked it. Wants us to get together someday and talk. Carl wants to finish the book, but I had promised it to Peter at the meat stand; so I'll take it back to Carl another day. Peter looked eager to have it, and I have a good feeling about him.

Many of the stall operators greet me now when I walk through, and I feel good there at St. John's Market. They seem eager to know about me and what I am doing here in Liverpool.

When I got back to 'Woolie's,' Mr. Little had gone home, so I chose to stay there for another hour. There were many Hare Krishna's in the area, but no one to stand for the Lord of Glory. Bless my soul if I'm not getting hooked on this thing.

On March 9th, I have an interview at the Liverpool Hospital, but am considering going into full time ministry by faith. But, if I don't get firm confirmation from the Lord by the ninth, I will gladly take the job. I see so much need all around me for ministering, teaching and helping that it sometimes blows my mind. I am ever mindful that He must guide and I must listen and obey. Praise God, it is such a joy to serve Him. I see Him much more clearly now and I love Him so much.

Must go to that concert, so I'll finish when I get back. That way I fall asleep with you on my mind. You would think I loved you or something, wouldn't you!

Midnight

The concert was nice but a little formal, so I just closed my eyes to enjoy it and almost fell asleep. Toward the end I really felt the presence of the Lord and was kind of sorry when it was over. The last couple of songs, people all over the place started to worship in the Spirit. I thought, "*Oh, God, why can't we allow you to minister and guide a meeting, instead of 'now, we'll sing this song,' etc.* " We gather in Jesus' name but leave Him in the back room, because He might do something silly and throw the whole show out of order.

Note: *I will begin to leave a few little endearments in so the reader can get a sense of the closeness my wife and I had during the two years I was in Liverpool.*

March 9th - 9 a.m.

Glory to God if I'm not the happiest man in the whole world! He gave me all of "you's" and all of himself, too. My hand was shaking as I made my cup of tea and toast and rushed back up to my room with my birthday treasure. How did you ever manage to time it so well? God is so good I would feel ashamed to ask for another thing the rest of my life. My heart is full with love for you. I want to express that love by walking for Jesus in town today.

Woke up about 3 a.m. this morning because of a bad dream, and stood looking out my window at the sleeping city. I told the Lord if He wanted to give me a birthday present, my wish would be for me to be His instrument that would ignite this city on fire for Him. I am well aware of the cost, but I shout in unison with Paul, *"But what things were gain to me, those I counted loss for Christ. Yes, doubtless, and I count all things but loss for the excellency of the knowledge of Christ Jesus, my Lord. For whom I have suffered the loss of all things, and do count them as nothing, that I may win Christ and be found in Him. Not having my own righteousness, but that which is through the faith of (in) Christ." Philippians 3:13, 14.*

4:00 p.m.

Had a strange day. I was excited on my walk through town when, suddenly, I got the feeling the Lord wanted me to take the sign off! It wasn't anything I had done, for I had never felt closer to Him. I just knew without a shadow of a doubt I was not to continue. I told the Lord I was willing to do it every day if He wanted me to; but, again, it was absolutely no. As I was taking it off, I felt a little sad because I had enjoyed it so much; yet, I was happy that my Lord could communicate to me so clearly. After all, hadn't I asked Him to show me His will for each day? Praise God, He cares so much for me. I went on the job interview at the hospital, knowing He went before me. It turned out well. I will know for sure in a couple of days. They didn't like the idea of my family being in the U.S., not being sure how long I'll be around; but, again, I'll just leave it all in His hands. Amen, Bella Rossiter? Do you know Jesus loves you more than the angels in Heaven? Did He die for them? Just think,

Bella, the secret that had been hidden since time began has been revealed unto us! *"Christ in you, the hope of glory!"* He is magnificent, and one day we shall see Him face to face. It's enough to give you goose bumps all over.

Last week I met a little boy downtown and it was an instant friendship. His name is Calvin, about ten years old, and he has the happiest face. I walked in to the cafe' facing Cousin's, Saturday, and there he was again with his dad. We had a good long chat. It turns out he has always loved America, for some strange reason. His room is full of things about the U.S. and he was thrilled to find out his new friend (me) was from there. I promised to bring him a real dollar bill on Monday (today) and give it to his mom, who works at the cafe. So today I went by there and his mom told me he was ill. He has epilepsy and takes fits quite often. She wants so bad to take him to Lourdes (Catholic). I shared how much God loves him and would heal him anywhere. There is no holier place than in your own heart. It is no accident that Calvin and I met. I made her believe with me that Jesus would heal him right at home. I showed her what I had written in my little book. *"Calvin – my little boy."* She was very touched. I'm sure Jesus is answering her many tears and prayers. I will pop in again tomorrow.

Tuesday, March 10th – Midnight

Got your Anniversary card this morning. Thank you, Bella. It was beautiful. I just lay here for a while thinking about you and me; how close we are, even from such a distance. You are like a special gift that will be enjoyed the best after all the guests have gone and the dishes put away.

It's raining outside but warm. Went to bed for a few hours with a cold and sore throat. Made me feel a little depressed. I didn't like that feeling, so I got up and went for a nice walk. The enemy sure knows how to come in like a flood, but I'm not having any of it. I sang my song, *"Lord, plant my feet on higher ground."* I'm thinking of starting a Bible study one night a week. Christians here don't seem to have too much desire to commit their lives in a deeper way. The study would be to evaluate where we are in the light of scripture, and to desire in our hearts to become what Jesus intended us to be. Otherwise, I would be wasting time and dishonoring God's Word. Also, thinking of one night a week prayer and fasting that God would break the hold Satan has on this city; and make us ready to minister and serve when the people are set free. I must challenge my own life more and more so that I can be a good channel for the Lord to work through, and be a good example for the younger ones.

Wednesday, March 11th – Midnight

I believe it is possible to have a church someday where people can come and feel the love, joy and peace of God, guided by humble servants of His who have been dedicated to ministering to the body and prepare them for the coming of the Lord. I have heard many times in recent days, *"You will never find a perfect church."* I say, Amen, but we can have one that is a lot closer to God's heart, even if we have to start one ourselves. All the Pentecostal noise will be gone, and in its place will be sounds of praise bubbling over from a heart full of love for the Lamb. People will not demand their rights as Christians, but lay them humbly at the feet of Jesus. Healing and blessings will come from the heart of God when He looks upon His children whose lives have been trusted into His care. There is so much to do now, Bella, that I'm not sure I have time for a full-time job. So many more important things than cooking. I want to live by faith, and yet I must listen for God's voice.

Just looked over at a picture of the five of you, and it all started twenty-one years ago today. I feel very proud and humble at the same time, knowing full well, without God's hand we would not be a family today. Your children, Bella, will *"surely rise up and call you blessed."* I pray you will sense the love I have for you the whole day through. Give everybody a big hug for me.

Monday, March 16th

Sunday night I got this urge to go see Jay Peek and what a fantastic time it turned out to be, Bella. He lives in a flat overlooking the River Mersey. He was delighted to think I would make the long trek in the rain with my flu just to see him. He has never opened up to anyone ever before. That night we were soon lost to the world and time as we shared from the depths of our hearts. Two people with complete trust in each other. I was so aware of mountains being removed to let the sun shine in, flooding his soul with a new awareness of God and what it really means to be a Christian. His whole life was an amazing paradox. The saddest thing of all was, after a whole year under the "faith" teaching, he never understood the meaning of a personal relationship with Jesus. The end result was emptiness and boredom to the point of quitting the whole mess. A distrust of all this Christian fervor with all the talk of love; yet, no one seemed to really love anybody, least of all him. He gradually retreated and could no longer even work up a plastic smile to match the group. All he wanted was to go back to being himself; at least that was real.

Bella, I pray that I'll always be a real person with real feelings. I don't ever want to be anything but what I am in Jesus. I want to throw away everything that could prevent another human being from finding peace with God. They are hurting and need relief from pain. Instead of giving them Jesus, we give them some cocky Pentecostal gibber. Instead of leading them gently to the Cross where we can lay our burdens down; then on to the empty tomb to see He is no longer there; for He has come alive to dwell in the hearts of His people. If we would only trust Him to do the changes, we Christians would find more time to just love and be the channel Jesus uses.

Did I make any sense, Bella? I'm not much good at putting it down on paper. Anyway, John will join us once a week for a Bible study. I know Jesus will meet him in a real way.

Yesterday (Sunday) I spent most of my time in bed with the flu, but I didn't mind. I was able to look at things and get a clear picture of people and needs, and see if there was anything I had overlooked to do for them. Rick came by for me to join them and another couple for dinner. It was about 8 p.m. and I was 'under,' but Rick said the couple, whom I've met a few times, wanted me to preach! I was out of bed in a minute, wasn't I? We did a beautiful study on the life of Paul and boy did God move! This man had "ants in his pants" and couldn't wait to ask Jesus into his life. While we prayed, his wife sobbed her heart out to see her husband, a big tough man, broken by Jesus. She had already done it in her quiet way. He couldn't sit down after that, but walked back and forth like a child on Christmas morning. He was so full, he had never hugged a man, and I was the first! He was so hungry, he begged us to stay and share. It was 2 a.m. when he reluctantly let us go. That makes six for the Bible study.

Bella, I didn't get the job at the hospital. They felt very shaky with you being over there and me not knowing how long I'll stay. But, I felt not one bit sorry. I would have had to work weekends and there are so much better things I could do. So, the life of faith seems to be the direction for now. I have no needs and I help Susan all I can. I work on the house as God supplies. Margaret gave me five pounds for my birthday, and I bought wallpaper for Susan's bedroom. She is tickled pink with that.

Peter the butcher, gave my book to another guy who has a stall in St. John's who wanted to read it. Peter wants me to come down today to talk, so I'll be on my way and finish this later.

Midnight

Peter had stepped out for a while so I got to share with his co-worker, Gary. It was hard going at first, but he warmed up to me and ended up wanting to read my book. Peter had talked to many people about the book because he had enjoyed it.

"But," he asked, "what is it, exactly, do you want me to do?"

I explained how God loves him, and through Jesus, has given us a way back to Him. Well, Peter couldn't see himself getting that involved. I said goodbye a few times, but he kept holding me with more questions. The poor guy had a battle going on inside, wanting to know more, yet not wanting to give me the idea he was interested. After I left I had the thought to give him the book, *"The Cross and the Switchblade."* I'll follow up on that and let God do the rest. I don't run after people anymore Bella, but I like to give them a fair chance to get hungry for more.

On my way home I ran into Sarah again. She told me how she had anguished day and night, crying to God for a way out. It all came down to the fact she didn't want the baby. On Wednesday it would be all over and she could get back to normal again. Bella, her mental suffering was so deep, I felt for her. I couldn't say one word that would add to her torture. I told her God loved her and He, too, could feel the anguish she was going through. The more I talked, the more I was sure God was speaking through me. The transformation in her was so complete that I marveled at my words of wisdom. It was God's love coming through me, soothing her aching heart. Then she said with conviction, *"I will have this baby just for God."* Praise His Holy Name! He loves us!

Tuesday Evening

Came home to find a letter from you. I hit the jackpot two days in a row! Thank you, Bella. I wanted you to get that special letter on our Anniversary, but it got there too soon. Honey, I did look for cards, but they didn't say what I felt. Then I thought of a telegram, but I was broke. Then I figured I'd call you, but that meant using someone else's phone in the middle of the night; and that last phone call was awful. I hoped my letter would do the trick in the end. If I had any idea you would end up with swollen eyes, a red nose and using half a box of Kleenex, I would have called you for sure.

I doubt if there is a person alive who can do anything to stop this country from total collapse. There's nobody working and there are factories closing down every day. But what a great place to be when you know you have the answer to all their heartaches and problems. God must surely move soon and we'll be ready for the greatest hour in Britain's history. One man by the name of Churchill rallied a whole nation from sure defeat to victory with nothing more than a gallant heart. What Jesus seeks is a godly man with a gallant heart who will wake up the defeated Christians to lay down their lives for God's finest hour. I do go on a bit, don't I, Bella. Bless you for hanging in there. It is not in vain.

Sarah walked into the hospital and walked right out again. God persisted through me and we now have a miracle baby on the way!

My heart's desire now is to wait and pray for the endument of power from on high, that God may shake the very foundations of this city. If this is the end result of my coming, I would gladly be spent for it.

Exhortation

> *"Church, you had better wake up from your slumber before the wrath of God comes upon you, for you have been trusted with much and given back so little. Remember, therefore, how great my salvation was to you in that day of visitation. Why do you now treat it as a gift, to be put away until such a time as polishing brass, only to be put away for another season. The life I shed was for all people, for all times and you stand idly by while the fruit rots in the field. The harvest is now, so put away your trinkets and return to the fields of your salvation, or I will remove your candlestick from my heart!"*

Thursday Evening

My dearest Bella,

I was up and out by 7 a.m. It was the kind of beautiful sunny morning that makes you want to walk forever. On my way out I bumped into the postman with a letter from you. I wanted to savor it for as long as I could, so I popped it in my pocket and had a glorious walk through Princes Park and on to Sefton Park and the boat lake. There, I sat down and was promptly entertained by a duck and six of the tiniest little chicks you ever did see. You could have put all six in the palm of your hand with room to spare. With the sun shimmering on the water and a gentle breeze blowing, I slipped out my treasure and almost fell off the park bench. To think I came that close to being a dad again. It gave me goose bumps all over. It would have been the most beautiful gift in the whole world. Well, after my dreamy thoughts had time to settle, I had to admit, God knows what He is doing! Right, Bella? But to think how well you took the whole thing was truly wonderful and I am very proud of you and love you very much.

My brother Joe came by to see me. He was feeling very low and disgusted with life. Seems someone had stolen his new ladders worth over $150.00 from the back yard of a house he was working on. Anyway, one thing led to another and after about an hour, he ended up giving his life back to the Lord. When he got home he found out the ladders were back in the yard! God does work in strange ways!

I had my first Bible study last night and it went off very well. My main aim is to encourage them to seek a personal relationship with Jesus instead of just believing in Him, so that when hard times do come, they can turn to Him. He must become the very foundation on which we rest our lives. Otherwise we go under at every shake of life.

Liverpool Bible Study Group

Now, Bella, I'm going to share something with you, but please don't get concerned; everything is in God's hands. A man named Rex came to kill me with a hammer last week. (*Not a hair on my head was harmed.*) He had been despondent over his daughter wanting to leave for the U.S. Even after he was told I had nothing to do with it, he still insisted I was trying to break up his family. He went out and got drunk and came knocking at the door at three in the morning. Thinking it was my brother, I went down in my shorts. When I opened the door, Rex was standing there and started cursing me. I didn't feel afraid, but I was shocked! In a calm voice I told him to come in, I'd put on some pants, and we could talk about it. As I turned to leave, I just caught a glimpse of him pulling something out of his coat pocket. I stepped backward and ducked just as he threw the hammer at my head. I walked back to the door, where he demanded the hammer back, or he would come in and get it. Susan was behind me holding a crying baby, so I got it and gave it back to him to keep him outside. He was a raving maniac. As he lifted the hammer to hit me with it, this is what he said,

"I hate you, going around preaching God. Well, I'm Satan and I've come to kill you!"

I reached up and grabbed the hammer in his hand. We stood there face to face, him screaming he hates me, and me telling him I love him. After what seemed an eternity, I let go of the hammer. He turned and started smashing the coal locker door outside. Finally, he started to walk away, still throwing abuse at me. I was able to close the door slowly and went back upstairs.

I knew in my heart I was no match for him; it had to have been God's divine protection. How else could I stand in my room without an ounce of bitterness toward him? I saw him as a lonely, bitter man who hates me for being all that he longed to be, but couldn't because he was locked in his own prison of self-pride. Satan found an easy vessel to put out the light, but the light overcame darkness, for that light is the Light of the world. *"Greater is He that is in me, than he that is in the world."* I prayed for Rex that night that God would set him free. I felt sure that someday I would see him go down on his knees and cry like a baby; and all the city would know that God had done a great work. I called him the next day, but he didn't want to talk to me. He has since found a job in London, so I will pray each day for a miracle.

Tuesday 11 p.m.

My lovely wife and friend,

Thank you for your letter this morning. I hardly expected it, because I'm still basking in the joy of the tape you and Debbie sent a few days ago. C.T. Studd must have surely been a great man to have been apart from his loved ones for so long. I wonder if I'll ever love Jesus that much! Isn't it wonderful you, Deb and I love the same Lord and walk the same path! I can feel a real deep bond of love growing between you and our Deb, and it's all built on our love for our sweet Savior Jesus. Debbie is headed for the Promised Land, and my joy has no bounds. Glory to God that you and I can see our daughter blossom like a rose. If only I could kiss you both just once, or hold your hands for a little while, how happy it would make me. I could go on with new strength. I just got a silly thought for her, ***"Don't take anything less than the real thing, and don't give any more than everything!"*** I must be getting old! Ha!

Let's keep our eyes on the City of God and leave Christian City far, far behind. Let's dig up the Old Rugged Cross again and get a few splinters. That new shiny cross they have these days keeps slipping out of my hands. It's made of light-weight aluminum, so it doesn't get heavy. The trouble is I tend to forget I'm carrying it, plus, I can't nail anything to it, it's so fragile. (Oh, dear, I am getting old!)

Rex is back from London already! Had a nice talk with his wife, asking her to give him a little extra praise once in a while, and do something special for him, even if you think he doesn't deserve it. He seems to be jealous of me because he feels a failure. Give him half a chance and he will respond.

Wednesday Morning

I'm down at Cousin's Bakery where you and I used to have a cup of tea together – three sips and it's gone, for sixteen pence, ugh. I'm not far from where Calvin's mom works, so I'll pop on in. Up to date, she has not been too friendly, being a Catholic herself. So, once again I have planted for another to water. Same with the men from the book stall and meat market. I have planted where seed has never been before; now I must leave it up to God. Each one is interested in the second part of my book. Maybe through that will come some deeper conviction. I feel ready to start writing again. Be in much prayer, as all hell will break loose to stop me.

Liverpool has a way of crushing the strongest heart. I feel a deep need to fast and pray for a week or longer, till I secure some answers to all the needs. I must find more time alone. I want to do battle with the enemy, but my flesh is weak. I will *"press on toward the mark of the high calling of God"* till I stand with one foot resting on Goliath. For when he is defeated, the whole army of Satan will run in fear. Who is Goliath? Sometimes I feel it's me, myself. And when I am truly dead, the Lord of Glory shall reign in this mortal body. His words shall pierce deep into the hearts of men. They will fear Him and tremble, for their sins shall be uncovered before that great and terrible day of the Lord. The last stronghold is me.

Well, Bella, my love. You remember I said I must die here, or I can't go on. This is the place I must find rest. When I am nothing, truly nothing, then God's mighty power can flow, touching, saving, healing, loving. Then the world will know that Jesus lives in the hearts of His people. He is risen, and may them that sing it, sing from a heart full of this knowledge. It is true! He has Risen! Don't ever think believing is enough, for the disciples believed and locked the door in fear – till He came and said, *"Fear not!"* And they saw him and died for Him and never looked back. They did not die for the empty tomb. They died for a Risen Lord who promised to be with them always, till the end of time.

Pray for me, Bella and Debbie. Not from your lips, but from the depths of your hearts. Be my intercessors and watch the spring blossoms turn to summer fruit. For this truly is the time of travail, followed by life – new life.

Sunday

My dearest Bella,

I realize, my love, that viewpoints can get distorted from such distances and different cultures. Reading Paul's life, *"My God shall supply all my needs."* And again, *"Whatsoever state I find myself in, therewith to be content."* Also, *"I have suffered the loss of all things."* Not least of all is my loss of nearness to you, my lovely family. Yet Paul was not lax in his rebuke to exhort them in love, to see the needs of their brothers, so that they (the givers) may grow thereby. That is my only purpose for writing and I pray you will receive it in the same mind as it is written.

I have had no money for weeks and even if I did, it would go for needs far greater than my own. But you are more apt to feel my needs before you would anybody else's; that is why I share mine and not another's. I walk everywhere in all kinds of weather; buses have become a luxury I can't afford. My one prayer for each letter I write is, *"Lord, I need a stamp."* That's why I laughed, Bella, when you sent me some English stamps. Only God could have known. But, I don't want to bore you or make you feel sorry for me, for I would not trade it for all the world's riches.

Enough of this talk. I have tried making a tape and failed, but I will try again tomorrow. Once again, I thank you and Deb with all my heart for your tape of love to me. I have listened to it four times and I feel a lump in my heart each time.

Saturday, April 4th – Midnight

My dear sweet Bella,

Thank you for your welcome letter. It was a ray of sunshine in my week of despair. I knew it would happen eventually. No matter how hard I tried, I could not stop the crushing defeat. It was one step after another starting with the stopping of the Bible study at Cody and Samantha's, then the prayer meeting on Saturday when no one showed up. Then a falling out with two of my closest friends. I couldn't wait to get to the safety of my room. I was totally empty. I looked out my window for a long time feeling alone like never before. Now I couldn't even turn to you for comfort, Bella, you were so far away. I felt you were the only one who has never stopped being my friend, no matter what. You have always been there when I needed you.

Note: *In retrospect, I believe my immaturity as a Christian brought on much of the above and more. I was like a bull in a shop full of fine China. I made many mistakes because I was acting alone, rather than in conjunction with a church or group of believers. In short, I needed a mentor, a godly man or pastor to whom I would be accountable.*

I lay in the dark for a long time, thinking. I had let the Lord down a million times, but never once my friends. I had shown only love and kindness. So, tomorrow is a new day! I will leave behind all my heartaches, along with the Bible study and prayer meeting. I will look for a fresh beginning; maybe closer to the Florie Boys Club (officially named Florence Institute Community Center) on Mill Street. I want to cut away anything from my life that may hinder God from moving, including my hurt feelings, and see which way the Lord wants me to move.

Our trials come, but the victory is in knowing He will never leave you nor forsake you. Let Satan pour his evil garbage on our pathway to the City of God. We will just trample it under foot and use it as stepping stones.

Well, my sweet wife. All is well with my soul, too. Another day is dawning and who but our God knows what new things it will bring with it. Let's you and I run the race to win. For Jesus' sake.

Sunday Morning

It's a perfect Sunday morning. So peaceful and quiet with the sun shining. I walked to the promenade and back by way of the two parks. The blossoms were in full bloom and I got to watch a football (soccer) match. Just finished giving Rex's daughter driving lessons.

She is doing just fine and her dad is now very friendly to me.

More and more I feel the need to be alone and do some deep reading. I only read my Bible now. Didn't even enjoy the two Dave Wilkerson ministry letters you sent me. Not sure why, but they never ministered to me, even though I read them with much expectation. God bless him, he is a real man of God. (*Psalm 17:15 and Proverbs 31:27, 28)*

Saturday – five minutes after we talked

My dear Bella,

I am high and lifted up in my spirit. I am beside myself with joy and ready once again to meet the challenge set before me. See what love can do! It is the greatest force in the universe, and has truly moved mountains for me. I have said it before, but it doesn't hurt to say it again, *"I am blessed of all men when God gave me you."*

I will stay here and learn of Him till I have put myself to rest. Never again will I allow Satan to run me out. God has proved over and over again that when I am at my weakest, He sends me an angel to minister to my needs. All glory and honor to such a sweet Savior. I have tasted but a small portion of suffering compared to His, and only now do I begin to understand the meaning of the power of His suffering. More and more I see Paul as my earthly father, teacher, friend. For he, more than any man, walked with Jesus in all his ways. *"Paul, two thousand years later, you are still begetting children to a lively hope. Praise God! For you were a faithful servant to the end. Your words were in weakness and fear and much trembling. Not in the wisdom of men, but in the power of God. Oh, that men would learn from you instead of the wise men of this world."*

Yesterday was a nice day. I walked through the Cathedral graveyard reading the headstones of those who passed on hundreds of years ago. My thoughts went something like this. *"Well, my friend, if you could speak to me now, what would you say? Would you tell me that death is the end and to live life to the fullest? Maybe get a good education and become somebody? Drink and be merry, and above all, don't talk about religion? Would you tell me to invest in real estate, get life insurance, and a good retirement plan, so I can relax in my twilight years? Or would you now say, be wiser than the wisest man, for I count it all as nothing that I may win Christ, and be found in Him. Were you trapped in man's religion or did you lay up for yourself treasures in heaven which you are now enjoying? I hope so. If I had a choice of headstone, I would want it to be, "For me, to live is Christ – to die is gain."*

Sunday, 1 p.m.

Bella, my love,

I am filled with joy from the Lord. I am full because He spoke to me. His voice is so good to behold. I can't express how much I love Him. My spirit is moving inside of me and I sang, *"Praise Him, all ye lands! Praise ye the Lord, for He is good!"* I have tasted of His goodness and it is truly good. Words can never express the fullness of my soul!

I went to that little Park Street Chapel with only a handful of old people in it. From the moment I entered, my soul was full of wondrous expectation, from where I know not of. But the guest speaker read *Matthew 21:23-46* and I hungered for every word of it. He kept repeating the line in verse 28, *"Son, go work today in my vineyard."* He kept saying it was for someone here. I knew all along who it was for, 'cause my heart was bursting with praise and thanksgiving. If only I had the liberty, I would have sang a new song. I felt like standing up and shouting, *"It's for me, for I am filled with the Holy Ghost!"*

After the service I shook the poor guy's hand almost clear off, and told him God used him to minister to me. He admitted having a difficult time putting the sermon together. I assured him every word was perfect. He was very pleased, but not half as much as me. Praise the name of the Lord, who is Holy above all the earth!

I must learn to be patient and let God prepare the way ahead. I must be like the hummingbird in the poem. Do you think God gave that poem to me, Bella? Do you know how much I love you? With every breath.

To My Lovely Wife and Friend

Oh, Lord, how long before the sweet
touch of Spring
awakens the tender bud.
Is it mindful of the time?
Does it realize that summer will be
here soon?

The hummingbird hovers over the
promise of a flower;
patiently waiting, knowing it is the
hour of new life.
It is ready to sing, but dare not sing
too soon,
for fear of disturbing the delicate
balance of Nature.

The sun shines but for a moment.
Is it now, with baited breath?
But, not just yet, the wind is telling,
as the clouds move overhead.

A little rain, a dew-filled misty
morning,
is still not reason for hope to fade and
die.
For the day will come and the
hummingbird
will sing again.

And the flower blooms its fragrance in
the air,
when nature, dressed as Queen in all
her glory,

will usher in a brand-new day for all
the world to hold,
and the pain of Winter is all but
forgotten.

April 10, 1981 ~ *II Corinthians 4:17*

Susan is preparing dinner and it smells so good from up here. Is there no end to God's goodness? David must have had a good time writing those Psalms to the Lord.

Dropped in on Rex and took a lively interest in his pigeons, which he races. He was eager to answer my many questions concerning the birds, and even made me a cuppa. Love breaks down all the barriers, right, Bella? So, all in all, the Lord was my portion. Who can know the minds of men better than the One who made them!

Tuesday Evening

I mailed you a letter today, having held it for two days in my pocket for lack of stamps. Never mind, God knows what He's doing. I just don't want you to walk back from an empty mailbox sobbing. But, sometimes, it's not my fault, is it?

Yesterday, I happened to be walking past the home of a local vicar mowing his lawn, when he called me over. We had a cuppa sitting outside in the sun for over an hour. As he shared with me, I felt like crying, for his heart was in every way like yours and mine. He confided in me things on his heart that he would lose his job over, if the church ever found out he felt that way. To put it in a nutshell, he feels the churches are the biggest hindrance of all in the furtherance of the gospel and saving souls. He wishes he could throw out everything and start fresh and go out to love and save these poor souls, and bring them to a church full of life and joy of the Holy Spirit. He said we have a poor resemblance of what was once meant to be a dynamic force that could shake whole cities. Now the Christians don't even want it.

Well, Bella, you know me by now. I had to ask him why he should fear for his job and not do what God would want instead of men. He said the Lord was doing a great work in the house Bible studies. They started with a few and its now over seventy people in six houses, all on fire for the Lord. He had to be careful in this growing time. It was so good talking to him, I ended up mowing his whole lawn. I went back today and did about two hours trimming and weeding. The poor guy doesn't know what to make of me, but I sure enjoyed doing it. Besides, I got a nice healthy sunburn on my face.

Got a bit of a shocker when a family member told me something he had never told anyone before...he didn't know what to make of it. One night, after painting with me on Falkner Street, he was walking home late at night feeling tired. Suddenly, he got this warm feeling all over his body. He said he felt a peace like he never felt before, like he was glowing all over. It was so good, he wished it would never end, but after about five minutes it was gone. I told him it was none other than the Holy Spirit ministering to him; God's way of saying, *"I love you."* He said he wished he could be a Christian without all the Bible studies and church and stuff, and he could still go for his pint and a game of pool. I told him, *"So does everybody else, but that kind of belief doesn't change anybody – you have that already in the Catholic Church. God is waiting till you can give it all to Him; nothing less will do."* Poor guy, he is fighting it.

Wednesday Afternoon

My dearest daughter Debbie,

The sun is just streaming through my window, and my heart is full of joy and praise and peace. Can anything be more wonderful than being a Christian and knowing God as our lovely Father? There is no joy to compare with the joy of the Lord. I thank him for this sunny room. I thank Him for the peace that passeth all understanding. But, most of all, I thank Him for you, whom I delight in with all my heart.

Tomorrow you will play the lead role in *Alice in Wonderland* to hundreds of young people. I pray right now that they will be captured by the beauty of the Lord in you. May this be a special moment for each of their lives as they say to each other, *"Didn't our hearts feel good when she spoke,"* for truly you are filled with the Holy Ghost, and He will shine His light into the hearts of the people.

Debbie, I just can't wait to get that tape with the funny story on it. How could you do this to me? And I will listen very closely to your special song. I wish I could hug you right now. Go tell your mom to hug you for me before I go crazy!

Thank you for relating me to your Heavenly Father, Deb. That goes for me too, when I realize He loves His children like I love mine; it is easy to love Him back with all my heart.

I bet that pimple on your nose looks cute. And the feet were very funny – tee-hee-hee. Well, Deb, the future is in God's hands for all of us. Walk each day in Him, that's all He desires. From that will come all the rest. One step leads to another, and without much fuss, we end up just where He wants us to be.

Easter Monday, 11 p.m. (*Isaiah 58:1-12)*

My dear sweet Bella,

After reading about Paul and the great men of God, I am beside myself with shame. The suffering they went through for the sake of the gospel made me cringe to think I complained of loneliness. May God give me another chance to redeem my pitiful self and get back to being a real man. I will never complain again, but will endure all things as a good soldier. Amen to that.

My Love

My walks in the park are only half enjoyment,
for my hand is empty, hanging by my side.
My footsteps linger only for a moment,
to gaze at scenes of Nature's handiwork.

Then on again, my eyes to drink the beauty,
my ears alive to birds in symphony.

But somehow I can't move my heart to join me,
for it has chose instead to be with you.

A shady tree has beckoned me to join her,
her solitude and coolness I decline,
for the luxury she offers is to daydream
of you, I'm sure, but no, I must go on.

But I'll come this way again another season,
and sit beneath your shade, but not alone.
My hand will hold another hand so tender,
with joy unlocked, my heart will know no bounds.

Frank ~ Liverpool ~ April 14, 1981

Well, Bella, my love. I do feel like this is a turning point for me. I honestly feel like I need to start telling people that, unless they get right with God and turn from their sins, they are lost and on their way to hell. It's nigh on impossible to turn this city from its deep wickedness, just by showing love and kindness. They also need to be awakened by a John the Baptist, or a Jonah, or Elijah.

I wouldn't mind if God would see fit to anoint me with such boldness. I am ever aware that such preaching should never be done outside of the power of the Holy Spirit, otherwise, I'd be in real trouble. But, I will pray for it till it comes. How this widespread wickedness can prevail with so many Christian churches around only goes to testify to their lack of this power. I can honestly see now, why we are not being persecuted for the faith. The sinner doesn't even know who we are. And if by chance they do, it's usually with a snicker as they watch us sneak into our little comfy nests called church, where we are told how much God loves us, and how wonderful of God to snatch us away from that wicked world outside.

So we sing three old hymns, hear a sweet sermon, give our offering, cough, and stay for a nice cuppa and a little chat before we sneak back outside, hoping the baddies won't mug us. Do we dare ask the sinner to give up his exciting life to join such a boring, powerless crew as us? I know I wouldn't. But, if you read in Acts chapter 5:12, you get a different picture. *"And by the hands of the apostles were many signs and wonders worked among the people. And of the rest durst no man join himself to them; but the people magnified them. And believers were the more added to the Lord, multitudes, both of men and women."*

I believe with all my heart that this is for us today. But, the price is very high. It will cost you everything. But, who is willing to pay?

Wednesday

Praise God for His unspeakable joy that I have in you, Bella. I am eager to go on after a blessed day yesterday. Once my eyes are back on Jesus things do change, not so much on the outward but on the inward. I am learning the sacrifice of me! Instead of dwelling on man's carelessness in hurting me, I have made up my mind to only bless them. The result was I became an encouragement to many that knew they didn't deserve it, yet responded to it with hunger. *That is God at work.* Anything else is not worth the trouble.

I have a feeling that our God is going to be glorified. Oh, for the complete death of me, that I might see His wonders performed more abundantly. Satan has tried to run me out, but I praise God for my weakness. For when I am weak, He is made strong. Where is your sting now, Satan? For God has beaten you at your crafty game, in a puny man such as me, no less!

Last night I told Susan's two little girls bedtime stories. One of David and Goliath and one of Joseph. When I kissed them goodnight, they said they loved Jesus and God a whole lot. I feel these memories will be used to draw them closer to the Lord when they get older.

I can say from my heart, I am at peace with all men. If I find such a time when I am not, then I will go with all haste, to make it so. I find pride to be the number one enemy with the Christian church. Kill that, and you have a church that has been truly set free to move as one body, one soul, one mind and one spirit. The power that will generate from it will turn this world upside down for the cause of

Christ. The enemy's biggest weapon is to keep us divided. A house divided *cannot* stand.

Saturday, 11 p.m.

My dearest Bella,

The phone call cost twenty pounds, but it was worth at least twenty million! I just got through reading your letter for the third time today, so I just needed to finish the day by saying, I love you very much. You are a pumpkin-head for saying I'm more romantic to you when I'm away; but I must admit there is some truth in that. Nevertheless, I'll have a jolly good go at changing all that in the future. Don't say I never warned you.

Went and ordered twenty tickets for the Nicky Cruz concert at a pound apiece. So it's all up to the good Lord to go before me, and get at least a dozen Florie boys eager to go for free. Talked to the Vicar of St. Gabriel's about transportation and there doesn't seem to be too much problem with that. I am excited at what our God can do with situations such as this. He is worthy to be trusted completely, so I am quite at peace with the whole thing. Isn't it great to be a Christian, Bella, and have our best friend be the Creator of this whole universe!

Last week the visiting pastor kept repeating the words, *"The Lord is about to do a mighty work in Liverpool."* After he said it a few times, he admitted not knowing why he said it so often. But I did! God was telling me to keep on going, for He is ready, willing, and able to do more than we could ever hope for. The only question I have is, *"Are we ready to give our all when God's mercy flows out to this lost generation?"*

Tuesday, 9:30 p.m.

Sunday morning after service, I approached Mrs. Bromley, the lady pastor, with a genuine smile of affection, for she is a very sweet lady. I asked her if it was time we had that talk. With obvious reluctance, she indicated we sit in the pew. I told her I was hoping for a little more privacy. She said, no, this was fine. Throughout our conversation, I spoke with much tenderness, yet I was firm, knowing she needed to hear the truth. It went something like this:

"Mrs. Bromley, why have you avoided talking with me?"

"But, I haven't. Is your last name Rossiter?"

"Yes."

"And, you've gone to Pastor Rowland's church?"

"I have in the past."

"Well, we're not Pentecostal here, and don't intend to be."

"Mrs. Bromley, I didn't come to talk about Pentecost. I came to help save the souls of these poor people that are all around us."

"There are plenty of Pentecostal churches you can go to, why here?"

"Mrs. Bromley, you continue to fill your mind with Pentecostal fear, when all I'm interested in is saving souls for Jesus. This morning, your opening prayer was so beautiful. You told the Lord that this chapel belonged to Him. That He would save the youth who are on the road to Hell. You prayed that God would bring a revival. Did you mean all that? Because, if you did, what do you think a revival would look like? Do you think for a minute a revival wouldn't set your place on fire with people praising and worshiping God for His mighty power and love in snatching them from Hell? If it did happen here, would you say, no, you don't want it, like you're saying to me, because you don't want to change the way you've been doing things for years? Your husband did a wonderful work, but that is over. God wants to do a new thing here. Look around you, what do you see? A dozen elderly saints. Do you think this is what God wants? Do you think it pleases Him to see us week after week, the same faces singing three old hymns and a short sermon while the world outside is on the road to hell? Are you waiting for them to come to you? Do

you think for a minute this is what they would desire to come to as a new way of life? Or would they much prefer to find a joy and love that would fill them, drawing them back each week for more?"

"I feel I have been insulted!"

"I only want to share the truth with you, Mrs. Bromley, but sometimes the truth does hurt."

"We don't pay anybody here."

"I would work twenty-four hours a day for free. Don't you realize I have left everything I love to come here, because I believe God wants to use me to reach these people. But, I need help. I need a place to bring them."

"Well, I'm sorry, but we do have plans for this chapel."

"Is it what God wants?"

"Well, I should hope it is!"

"So do I, Mrs. Bromley, I hope so, too."

Well, Bella, you know only too well how those kind of confrontations leave you a little drained and sad. But, you know, I felt such peace as I walked home. I prayed that God would be with her and minister healing to her broken spirit. I had spoken only in gentleness and love and felt the Lord was pleased. The rest of the day and evening I spent alone in my room, in fellowship with the Lord. It was great to sense His presence the whole time and just enjoy talking with Him and reading the Word. Praise filled my heart with the wonder of Him. I had conversations with Him like never before. I knew in the depths of my soul I would never feel alone again! He is my Friend, Bella! Sounds simple, I know, but when He got through with explaining what that meant, it was enough for me.

Praise His Holy Name!

Monday I made a sign for the Florie, with the offer of a free trip to see Nicky Cruz for the first dozen boys who signed up. This was two in the afternoon. Five minutes later I had eleven names and the Florie doesn't even open till 7 p.m. I went back today to check it out but someone had torn it up. When I talked with the youth leader, he said there was way over a dozen names on it. Bella, there may be as many as thirty kids wanting to go; so, I'm going to take every last one of them! Praise my God for being so faithful. I am full of faith that He is ready to do great things for us here. I am finding it difficult to get one mini-bus; now I need two and there's only one day left. I am confident in my spirit that God does all things well. I am at peace and my joy knows no bounds. The Lord loves us all! Thank You Father, for you are worthy of all praise and honor and glory. You are so rich in goodness. You are smiling upon us and it feels so good. We want nothing else but You. I want my Father to be happy!

Wednesday, 9 a.m.

Praise God! Your letter was waiting for me when I got home. How can I tell you how I really feel except to say I am filled up! I have need of nothing. I am blessed deep within my spirit, my cup is full! I want to bless my God for giving me such a joy in you. I want my sons to know I love them so much. I hurt for Frankie. I know what he's going through and want him to let go and let love come in. Love, joy, and peace are at his very fingertips, yet, if he doesn't reach out to take hold of it, it may as well be a million miles away. I wish I could take his hand and do it for him, but I know I can't. So, I suffer in silence, praying for the day when he will break, and the floodgates will open wide to wash away all the hurt and bitterness. Then the precious Son will come and shine in his soul; and Frankie will say, as we all have said, *"Why did I wait so long?"* If I could get you to do it by begging, Frankie, I would, but there is nothing I can do, just love you.

And you, Jimmy. What will you do now that you are out of Manna? Will your faith hold? Do you have your feet planted firmly on Jesus, or will you now drift back to the world that hates everything that is good? Now the real test begins for you; which way will you go? One way will give you pleasure for a season, but will destroy everything that is good in you. The other way will give you life, and make you a blessing to the world you live in. There is so much heartache and sorrow all around us, Jim, and you could be used by God to bring healing to them. Make your stand for God and never look back. I love you.

What can I say to you, Tony? You have been such a faithful son, and I am very proud of you and your accomplishments. I delight in telling people of your determination to make a success of your life without any help from anyone. Yet, when I'm alone, I can't help thinking all your good effort will never bring you peace in your heart. The world will look at you someday and pay you honor at your success; but, you and I know, it will be empty and hollow in the end. For, like every good play, the director is looking for only one thing – the response after the last curtain goes down. It is only out of love I can even dare talk to you this way, and I know you love me enough to take it from me.

Note: *I have purposely left in the above letters addressed to my children to give the reader a glimpse into the personal struggles my dear wife was having to contend with while I was off trying to save other people's children. It seems ironic I know, and many times I had to wrestle with the guilt that I wasn't there to help them. There is no excuse that would adequately explain why it was this way. I have to leave that part up to God and plead guilty.*

Friday Morning

It is over and my heart aches a little. Yet my spirit tells me not to judge too soon. *For His ways are not my ways.* Thank God He is patient with us. I ended up with fourteen boys. There were many hindrances up to the last minute of departure, but the Lord will forgive them (Christians) for their lack of faith and commitment to help. There were a few who stood up to the challenge. They are the real spirit of God, and to them I will be forever grateful. Bella, what I am about to tell you is from a heart that was filled with great wonder and expectation at the prospect of God's power being manifest through Nicky to these boys who have never experienced God's love at work.

Bella, his accent is still so strong, even I, knowing the story already, could not understand half of what he was saying. Plus, Central Hall was so large, his voice sounded hollow and echo-y. Within fifteen minutes I knew he had lost the interest of most of the young people. They squirmed in their seats and started to move around, talking to each other. I'm not just talking about my own boys, either. His story was flat and uninteresting; far short of the gripping story in the "*Cross and the Switchblade.*" He labored with it like he'd recited it so many times, even he didn't think it was worth telling one more time. There were many leaving for the 'bathroom'. One by one, my boys came over to me with the sympathetic voice to assure me they, too, were going to the toilet, and not to worry, they would be back. But, some didn't come back till near the end, and I couldn't blame them. My whole body ached as I sat there confused and bewildered, not knowing how or why this thing with such promise should turn out so bad.

If I had been alone, I would have left, too. I found myself praying for God's power to hold things together; that through it all, He would still manifest Himself in a real way to those hearts hungering after Him. The first altar call ended with a dozen going forward out of two thousand. Then he started to talk like he should have done all along; and I felt the Holy Spirit move. We sang a chorus, and I lifted my hands to praise my God. It didn't matter who saw me! God was at work. Praise His wonderful Name. People started to move till there must have been a couple of hundred out front, *including three of my youngest!*

After we got settled in the van, I asked for their attention and said, *"I want to thank all of you for coming. I know many of you found it hard-going sitting through it all. I think you did it out of respect for me, and I thank you for that. Nicky Cruz wasn't what you would call a good speaker, and his accent and the acoustics didn't help any. But, God was there, because I felt Him and so did many others. Those people who went forward by the hundreds didn't go because of Nicky Cruz, for they couldn't understand him any more than you could. But, let me tell you, if he spoke in Chinese, there would still be people going forward, because God does the work of touching hearts, and that's what it's all about."*

We got back by 11 p.m. and I went to work as caretaker, glad to be alone with my thoughts and heavy heart. I found myself praying for Nicky and his ministry, that God would give a fresh vision of Himself. Also, to heal his broken foot. He is my brother who needs much prayer, for this land is a hard place to minister. He must learn to *let go and put all his trust in the power of the Holy Spirit* to work out all the details. He must never depend on his story alone to grip people; for that will never be enough. He must learn to put his story of long ago aside, for it may not be appropriate for all occasions. He must learn to use the Word of God, *which he never did once,* and share what his God is doing with him today. May God bless this man, for I love him and I will hold him up in prayer. *For my God shall perform that which He has chosen to do. And He will do it with the foolish things; for even His foolishness is far, far greater than the wisest plan of the wisest man.*

I bow my knee once again to such a loving God. I determine in my heart never to look back on a situation without looking for the wonder and blessing in it for all. For who am I to even suggest that God did no mighty work last night. I am so puny, I can't even begin to see the Spiritual depth of love that was poured out, or the victory celebration of angels that went on last night. I am so small, I want to vanish, that I would never be seen again; that our great God and Savior may be all in all. *"My soul doth magnify the Lord, and my spirit hath rejoiced in God my Savior. For He that is mighty hath done great things, and Holy is His Name."*

I love those boys at the Florie, but my puny efforts are nothing compared to what God is doing by His Spirit.

Tuesday, 11 p.m.

Hello, my lovely Bella,

It was so good to hear from you this morning. I was up at 6 a.m. just to wait for the mailman and you never let me down. Thank you. I was in real need and it lifted me up.

After reading your letter, I walked to town and had myself a cup of tea. I just sat there enjoying the early morning and thinking of you. I went ahead and purchased some cute curtains, a lampshade and a beautiful poster to finish off the girls' room. Bella, it looks like a picture postcard in there now. Susan and the girls are delighted with it, and gave me a big hug.

Well, Bella, I thought that was reward enough for me, but then Winsome came by this evening. She told me the Lord very clearly instructed her to give me a gift. Now I can buy my shoes, as the others have gone kaput. He knows what we have need of before we can even ask. Thank you, Lord!

Starting tomorrow, I am heading for the room at the Florie early to pray through till I start getting some answers. I feel at times that I am failing miserably, and it all boils down to total commitment. My whole life should be given to seeking after Jesus, and waiting upon Him in prayer and fasting till the Spirit comes. *My spirit is willing, but my flesh is weak.* Why is it so hard to do? If we know there is treasure there, why aren't we digging till we find it? If the only thing that turns a man's heart to God is the Holy Spirit, then why do we go around frustrating the grace of God with everything but the Holy Spirit? We are playing games, and I am the worst offender. I have more time than most, yet I spend it so unwisely. It is clear I will labor in vain, unless I sacrifice all my time, my thoughts, my very life to seeking after the power of God that His mercy may flow through me to this Godless generation. No great preacher, no great testimony, no great anything will ever change one person, unless it is done by a vessel filled with the Holy Ghost and power. I am sick of standing and singing another hymn. It is worthless, meaningless, unless I am filled with God's love. Why can't we spend time in God's presence first; then, from a heart that's full, we can open up and never want to stop. Praise God, and Lord, please forgive us, we are so carnal and shallow. I don't want to feel ashamed when I stand before You to behold you face to face and recognize fully who You are and what You have saved me from. I know even now that in that day I will long for another go at it. For You are great beyond words and worthy of every ounce of my being. I am selfish and not even good material to work with. I tear easily.

Well, Bella, they say what you confess you possess; but I say unless we confess we don't possess anything. We had better start confessing how worthless and useless we really are without His divine love filling our very being every moment and start throwing away some of the garbage we are being fed to win this world with. There are few saints who are dying for the faith, while the vast majority sit in plush castles, singing, "How Great Thou Art," *to me...*

Was supposed to do volunteer work at the Florie starting tonight. But they closed it down in retaliation for the kids breaking into it last night and stealing valuable equipment used for photography classes, and broke quite a lot of things beside. The youth manager just shook his head in bewilderment at the gross destruction of their very own club. I told him only the hand of God could change such wicked hearts, like He did mine. He answered, *"That would be a welcome sight, indeed."*

So, tomorrow I hang the sign for a Bible study, with such eye-catching questions as, *"Is there really a Hell?" "Are we close to the End of Time?" "Can you know for sure you are saved?" "Does God still work miracles?"* etc. Now it's up to the Lord to go before me. There is one guy respected by all the youth who can be a good leader to the rest. He showed a keen interest in the End Time events. I bought him the *"Late Great Planet Earth,"* last week. Let's hope and pray for such a one to come alive and lead the way.

Hope I didn't bore you, Bella. Sometimes I wonder at some of my letters, but I do try to write as I feel. Sorry, no poems this time. Got a feeling that's all you're going to get.

Interesting sidebar:
Liverpool is changing rapidly. Every time they knock down old houses, they make little parks out of them with lots of trees. There's a big stink about it because there was always a shortage of housing; now there's an even bigger one. One of the headlines in the paper was, ***"Soon all of Liverpool will be camping out in our little parks, for they will replace all our homes."***

Tuesday, May 12th

My dearest wife and friend, Bella,

I suffered through the long weekend without hearing from you. Monday morning brought relief of my 'pain' with a lovely letter from you and my Deb. But, lo and behold, before I could finish off a reply, the lovely postman (I think I'm falling in love with that guy) deposited another one in my door this morning. I decided to start fresh, and I'm now in town at my favorite restaurant. I can sit for hours with one cup of tea till I finish this. The main post office is just around the corner.

I cried many bitter tears last night at what seemed like my puny effort to get things going here for the Lord. I thought of all the great men of God who had the ability, in one form or another, to get things done. It just felt like my inadequacy overwhelmed me. Then you sent Dave Wilkerson's letter!

We are all helpless before the Lord and that is exactly where we should be. If it means going out with nothing and ending up with nothing, what is that to me? Dying to self even means not caring about the outcome! He may prove me nothing by giving me nothing, but all praise and glory to Him if that should happen. My heart goes out to Dave in his hour of suffering over his lovely family. He has proven himself to be a man of God by going on in the face of such adversity. Are there other such treasures as he? Is his God not well-pleased with such a lively stone as he? Can I be one? Oh, how I hate to say 'prove me', for my love for my family is so deep. But, 'prove me' is what I have to say if I truly trust Him. For my God is lovelier than the spring morning and His promise of summer is surer than a budding tree. His love and perfect goodness should be all that we need to see us through all our trials and sorrows. *I Trust You, Lord!*

Well, Bella, I see a lot of 'movement' and many signs of encouragement in my daily rounds, but it would take quite a bit to explain them all to you. Just know that it is worth the sacrifice you and I have made. We walk by faith, therefore, we see all things through the eyes of faith. We believe God for all, or we believe Him for nothing. There is no easy way of winning souls. They all have to be wrestled away from the hand of Satan, one by one. The early church paid the price, and the price has never gotten any cheaper. It costs you everything!

Thursday, May 14th – 10 p.m.

Bella,

I have a confession to make; I blew the whole hundred pounds on clothes for myself. Now, you know how hard that must have been for me; but I was in such need. I began to look like a vagrant and needed a new outfit to give me a fresh lift to my sagging spirit. Oh, it felt so good to dress up tonight and go to a meeting at Maranatha. I spent four solid hours shopping to be sure I would come away with the best deal I could with yours and Debbie's hard-earned money. I think you would have been proud of me. It goes without saying, the pounds may just as well have been dollars in relation to what you can purchase with it. I ended up with a sports jacket, slacks, belt, shoes and socks. (I will try to fight the women off as best I can!)

Isn't it a great feeling when you're hungry for God, Bella, and He fills you? Oh boy, did that second Murillo tape you sent leave me spellbound. There's been times when I've felt that deep awareness of God's greatness, love and glory and His magnificence; He is all in all and there is none to compare. I was so thrilled with it! I took it downstairs to four of my (seven) sisters who were visiting and let them listen to it while I took the two babies for a long walk.

When I got back they were discussing how wonderful it would be to go to a meeting like that. I explained that that's what God intended all His meetings to be. Man, being afraid of the unusual and unexpected, pack Him neatly into a set of formalities where He can be controlled and explained; killing off the very life of the Spirit that has the only access into man's heart, drawing him into a relationship with God. All we'll have left is a place to go where we can hear stories about Jesus, but won't get the chance to meet Him in all His glory.

There will come a day, Bella, when we will have a church here, where people will exclaim, *"I see the Lord! He is high and lifted up and His train fills the temple!"* The gates of heaven will be opened wide and we will taste of the goodness of the Lord. We will be transformed into an Army that will turn this wicked city upside down; not by the fear of Hell, but by showing them the beauty and glory of the Lord of Heaven and earth.

Wasn't that a tragedy, Bella, the Pope being cut down like that? Man, did Dave Wilkerson's opening statement come back to me, *"In recent months I have had a sinking feeling inside me; a feeling that our entire society is spinning out of control, unraveling and falling apart."* When I saw the shooting on the six o'clock news, I flew up to my room to pray for him. I cried like a baby over this sick world that a loving God has to put up with.

In the midst of my prayer time, a great thunder and lightning rent the sky and the heavens opened up. It dumped a torrential downpour that lasted for a good half hour. I felt the depth of God's anguish at the wickedness of His creation. I told Him He had every right to terminate us there and then. I wouldn't blame Him a bit. But God's love is beyond our understanding. His arms are still outstretched, and so He waits still, while they kill His prophets and blaspheme His name. But, His judgment will come, and it will be swift and just. I ended my evening singing praises to Him for He is good, and I love Him.

Friday, 11 p.m.

Visited a youth club that I had discovered on my walk today. Had a great conversation for a full hour about Jesus with two leaders. I came away feeling so lifted at how the Lord put it all together. I'm sure there will be fruit from that. This kind of thing happens all the time; it's just hard to put it all into detail. But, take my word for it, it will all ripen in due season. Praise His Holy Name.

I am making a list of all the names that show promise, and lifting each one up daily in my special hour at the Florie. "I will pray them into God's family."

I have been given an open invitation to another youth club in the Dingle where I have shared more than once to a very receptive group of boys. More and more, I find myself being accepted by youth, but it has taken time. Patience and waiting upon the Lord seems to be the key elements here. Also, trying not to plan everything out, but walk by faith that God is going ahead of me. Last, but not least, not to get discouraged when you run into what may seem like a dead end. Just believe God to be working out all the details; His way, and in His time.

Monday, May 25th

Bella, my love,

It's 4:30 a.m. your time and I'm aching to call you. I don't think I will, for fear of running up another large bill. I haven't heard from you for such a long time (six days). I miss you and the fellowship we have when we walk and talk or just go for breakfast together. There is so much to talk about. It's impossible to put in a letter, because it's a thousand small incidents. Each one is insignificant in itself, but together, *it's the hand of the Lord!*

Praise His wonderful name for being so personal to me. He is far more precious than silver and gold, to be sure, and I want to plunge right in. This body of mine sure is a hindrance to me. I can well understand why we groan in our spirit to be released from its demands. We could pay more and more attention to the things of our great God and Savior Jesus Christ, the one and only true God who is lovely to serve, if we only could.

I used to wonder how angels could worship Him day and night, but I think I understand in part now. If we sometimes glimpse Him and rejoice, think what it would be like to be in His presence with nothing of mortal man to hold us back. I want to honor my God, but I am so weak. He is ever faithful, and I am so unfaithful to Him.

So many times I take the easy way when He went all the way, and wants me with Him. That way becomes increasingly narrower each step you take toward Him. But, He went first to show us the way, and said, *"walk ye in it." "In Me, all things are possible to them that believe."* When the way gets harder, it is time to shed yet another part of our burdensome load; otherwise, it is impossible to go on. The highway to the Heavenly City is strewn with the debris of man's lost state. There's a special point where man must shed his last burden, *Self.* The road is clear and the City brighter than the noonday sun. The only thing left to carry is our garment of righteousness, which shields us from the brightness of His glory. We feel no pain or sorrow, for we left it all behind. The road we traveled was Jesus, for our feet were on the Rock, on the Highway, for He is the Way. And all the time we never moved, for we were ever in Him.

Well, Bella, I was about to say, *"Where did all that come from?"* But I won't. I pray to God, Bella, that you don't think me more spiritual than I am. God forbid, for I am becoming more aware of how I really am. Whatever is done, or about to be done, is in spite of me. I don't even need a thorn in the flesh. Paul was worthy of the thorn; I never will be. However, I do want God to be shown in all His glory, for He is the bright and morning Star. None of us is worthy of such a love as His.

Yet, in spite of it all, He says, *"Come unto Me, all you who are heavy laden, and I will give you rest."* Just like a Father who sees us only as His children, and not the brats we really are.

There was a three-day Crusade at Central Hall. I went down Saturday afternoon to check out the times. They had an afternoon Bible session going, so I went on in. Man, Bella, I was blessed deeply by God. I went forward in response to a call to dedicate my life to the Word of God. I believe I received that anointing. I still wanted to ask the speaker for prayer; for what, I don't know.

Meanwhile, a man approached me and said the Lord had told him to pray for me from the moment I walked in, and he felt God had His hand on me. We became instant friends, and I'm sure we'll have much fellowship in the future. When I finally asked the speaker to pray for me, he laid a hand on my back and nearly burnt a hole right through, it was so hot! He took the longest time before he prayed, and I realized it wasn't a prayer but a prophesy from God to me. In essence, it was for me to stop striving and let Him do the work, and He gave me gifts to enable me in it. I walked home beside myself with joy and wonder at Him. After much trying to get others to join me, I ended up going back alone that night. The spirit of worship was a delight to behold and all the people entered in with the greatest of ease. It was truly one mind and one body.

There was a different speaker that night and, lo and behold, if it wasn't the prosperity message. I could have died. I prayed, *"Lord, why have you done this to me? Do you want to humble me so I can accept this teaching as from You? Have I been stiff-necked all this time? Then let me learn, if this is what You want me to do!"*

So I listened, Bella, with an open heart. At the end I was no more convinced that this was from the heart of God than before. I walked home with a heavy heart. *"Why, Lord, did you lift me up so high this afternoon to be brought so low only a few hours later?"*

(In contrast, Jesus says: "If anyone wishes to come after Me, he must deny himself, and take up his cross and follow me." Matt. 16:24. The prosperity message is to claim all the blessings of God in the form of the things of this world; money, fine homes, etc. There's nothing wrong with asking and receiving blessings from our wonderful and caring God so that we may be able to further the gospel and bless those around us who are less fortunate. The problem comes when we make it the central theme of all of our preaching and forget the other part which says, "I am crucified with Christ, nevertheless I live, yet not I, but Christ liveth in me. And the life I now live in the flesh I live by the faith of the Son of God who loved me and gave Himself for me." Gal. 2:20. In Galatians 6:14, Paul goes on to say, "But, God forbid that I should glory, save in the cross of our Lord Jesus Christ, by whom the world is crucified unto me, and I unto the world.")

I was, by now, totally confused. Was my heart closed to this teaching, when it should be wide open? After all, weren't they men of God, filled with the Holy Ghost, while I was such a little peon with little or no knowledge to preach or teach? But, the way they used those Scriptures left me a little uneasy, and what was the end product? *Me!* When I was desperately trying to get rid of *me!* So, I went straight to bed, glad to have a place to hide.

This morning was a holiday; there wasn't a soul moving when I went out at seven. I headed for the park, where I took shelter from the rain in an outdoor hut. Soon, another guy came along, and seeing me, excused himself and walked away. I ran after him and said, *"Hey, it's all yours, I'm through."* We looked at each other, and we both knew we were Christians. We walked in the rain together, marveling that we were the only two in the whole park, heading for the same little hut. I had not said anything beyond the usual greeting, when out of the clear blue sky, (not literally, it was still raining) he started to share his experience at Central Hall on Saturday evening. Up to a point, the service was moved by God, till the speaker forsook the mind of God to do his own thing, and labored in vain. My mouth was open and my heart was racing. Could it be I wasn't wrong? Could it be I wasn't the only one feeling a loss? Was this man sent to me for just this moment? The chances of this being a coincidence is just too great to even contemplate.

Sunday, May 31st – Midnight

My dearest Bella,

Can't go to sleep till I write a little to you. I seem to miss you most on Sundays, especially if I don't hear from you by Saturday post.

Found myself *walking by faith, not by sight* these last few days, but God restored unto me the joy of my salvation; it feels so good. Bless Him for His kindness in bringing me through. I can't wait for the morning mail to see how you are doing, Bella. Did I ever tell you how much I love you? More than anything in the whole world. You are a silent witness of God's love as people, time after time, ask me how my wife feels about this whole thing. I am only too happy to share how God has given us such a peace and oneness that is nothing short of a miracle. Thank you for being more than any man could deserve or hope for in a wife and mother. Heaven has recorded it for all time.

Monday Morning

No letter, Bella! Guess I'll survive one more day. I'm downtown waiting for the bank to open, so I'm having my cuppa. Jim R. sent me a gift. May God bless him for being so kind. It was one hundred pounds short of what I needed to buy the cutest mini-bus. But Joe, (one of my three brothers), has offered me exactly that much without knowing any details. God, You are great! Of course, that's besides what I intend to give to Susan for my keep. It is of the utmost importance that I stay a good witness to my family, and paying my way is at the top of my list. Plus, I have enough to buy more paint. My God has supplied all my need, and I want the world to know!

Been invited to speak to a youth group Thursday. Can't wait! Have an offer to have dinner tonight with a leader of St. Gabriel's Church. Seems like he is ready for change and is impressed with my approach to God's moving of today. God forbid that I have given reason to think I have anything at all! It is simply living out my experience as a Christian without hindrance of man or church. Yet God has led me into the church because I need the fellowship, and to see firsthand what it is that makes it what it is. I have learned that most of God's people are hungry for a deeper walk, but are unable to know what to do about it. We are all sick and tired of hearing of the great and glorious God in the pages of history, and yet settling for so little ourselves. Our hearts are burning for the living God, while the scribes describe and the elders get older!

Later

My lovingest, sweetest, kindest, beautifulest Bella,

With the phone conversation last night and a loving letter this morning, I am totally full of love for you and my God. I am rich! Who can know such fullness of love that I now feel, except the One whose love it is; the Lord of Glory!

After reading your letter, I sat back in bed and our Lord filled me with the sweet thoughts of victory. His love can never be expressed in words, but in thoughts of me holding you in my arms for a thousand years; to comfort you with the Spirit of Jesus. He is asking me to tell you, my love, to rest in Him. Step back and take hold of His hand and see from His perspective, the joy He has in store for you, and Who it is that is holding all things together.

He cannot trust just anybody with the treasures He has entrusted with you! *"Have I not said, and will I not perform that good work I have started in you? Fear not, it is my Father's good pleasure to give you the kingdom. I have overcome the world! Walk ye in my Love."* The secret hidden from all the ages, is made known to you, Bella. *Christ in you, the hope of glory!*

Spoke to fifteen youth at an after-church house meeting. None were Christians, but came for the fun and games each week; just another example of Christians doing good works. They lack the guts to level with these kids about their souls. I got stuck in and leveled with them, and they loved it! Bella, why do we act like we're ashamed of the Cross? Why can't we get it through our heads, it is the only thing worth speaking about! Why do we have to sneak it in like a tasteless medicine that has to be sugar-coated? It was a fantastic time, and I'm sure not one left the same as he came in. Praise the Holy name of Jesus, who teaches us to be true to His name. The youth are from St. Philemon's on Windsor Street. Keep them in your prayers.

Sunday Night

Went to St. Gabriel's this morning but left early. Feels like I'm coming down with something, plus the service was Yuk! More like a children's Sunday school. Went to St. Philemon's tonight and you wouldn't believe the warm welcome I received. Seems like the word got around about the success of the youth meeting Thursday. Met Doris R. there. She shared with such love how my wife (you) led her to Jesus and longs to see your smiling face again. She shared how her husband said it wouldn't last, but it's been over six years and getting better every day. Praise the Lord!

Tuesday Midnight

Note: *This next chapter is about Kent, a young man who wanted to join me here in Liverpool. He was a delightful Christian I'm sure would have been a great witness to the youth of this area and a great help to me in the Lord's work.*

You will never believe it, Bella. I'm sitting on a train in Lime Street Station, Liverpool, heading for London to rescue Kent out of the airport jail. I was at the Liverpool airport all set to pick him up when my brother showed up with the news that Immigration wanted me to phone down. That was the beginning of a six-hour ordeal of phoning and counter-phoning, till finally they decided Kent had to go back (to the U.S.) at 11:30 in the morning. He is in a holding cell, unable to talk to anybody. The main problem seems to be that I am unemployed, living with a sister who is on welfare. Kent can't work, no means of support, and has a one-way ticket. When asked how long he intended to stay, he answered, 'indefinite', making him a liability and not a holiday visitor. Nothing I said made any difference, so I'm heading down with every scrap of information I could find; letters of recommendation from pastors and youth leaders. Plus, *a God who formed the worlds with only a word.* They just don't know who they're messin' with, do they, Bell!

In the midst of all this, while my sick body was sagging under the phone ordeal, I got a wonderful letter from you, which perked me up some. Will you ever quit being an angel? The train is rocking too much to continue with this. I'd better not send it till Kent is safely home with me. Otherwise, you'll go out of your mind wondering at the outcome. I wouldn't do that to my best friend. Have a whole compartment to myself, so I'll try to get some sleep...

Thursday, 4 a.m. – June 11th

Was able to see the official about 8 a.m., and for the next hour went over everything with him. I laid it all out so plain and simple, I expected him to break down and cry any minute, but he came back in ten minutes and informed me their decision still stands. I was stunned. How could they be so pig-headed and empty-hearted? I had presented Kent, beyond a shadow of a doubt, as a man who sold everything he owned to come here and work with troubled youth. While here, he would be supported by the whole family, sponsored by two pastors and two leaders of boys' clubs, plus five hundred dollars in his pocket. I presented proof of purchase of a mini-bus for youth work, and my ability to survive without any of their handouts. Plus, a whole range of people who would gladly give their stamp of approval on the work I have done. *It was as if they were blinded!*

I did get to spend a couple of hours with Kent and we had a wonderful time. He was in good spirits as we planned our next move. We knew this was but the beginning of a hard battle to win God's people back to Him. Faith can only be tested in the fire.

When Satan puts up such a fight, it can only mean you are stepping on his toes. God allowed this to happen for a purpose. Was it to strengthen our faith and will to fight? For I would rather fight alongside a veteran than one with a diploma in his hand. *II Cor. 4:7-12. Romans. 8:35-37.*

Midnight, Friday – June 12th

My dearest sweet Bella,

Just a few thoughts to you my love, before my eyes give out. Had a good chat with Mark D. this morning. He wanted to know if I was 'in' with him or just hanging loose, as they have considered me for visitation ministry. I told him I would be delighted with such an outreach. I consider his church my home, so long as my hands are not tied to move in other areas, as I feel the Lord directing me. He gave me his blessing and will also write a recommendation for me on behalf of Kent, to welcome his contribution. I will send it on to Kent to enhance his chances of passing through Immigration, as a missionary of sorts.

Went to see Reg Ash from the Florie. He wanted to know if I would go with him on a week's retreat as the driver of a second mini-bus. This would be for needy families of the area, not the youth of the clubs. I would be fully involved with all aspects of it. He even pointed out the place we were going had a small chapel that would be at my disposal. When I told him the Lord had given me a mini-bus, so there was no need to rent one, he was shocked and very impressed. He asked me if I got any supplementary benefits at all, and I said, *"No, none."* He was silent for a long time, then said, *"Remarkable!"* I told him of my plans to take sixteen (keeps going up, I can't say no to anyone) boys on a week's camp-out to Wales at ten pounds a head. He didn't think that was enough, and would look into some way of helping with the finances, so I wouldn't end up the loser. He, too, will write a recommendation and an open invitation to Kent. Who can know the mind of such a God we serve? I have quit asking why things happen the way they do. I would rather stand back and say, *"This one is all yours, Lord!"*

Saturday

I'm downtown with my little cuppa. The morning sun is shining through the window.

Seems like my sister has been waiting for me to start up a fellowship and has built up a resentment to my free wanderings. I told her I walk one day at a time and will never again feel pressured into starting anything. Whatever I do will be the result of my walk. I am at peace with or without a church. I told her she must find that peace too, in her relationship with Jesus on a day to day basis. Not wait till Sunday night for some church to give it to her. I reminded her that I come faithfully to have fellowship with her, only to find unrest and resentment at life. I told her I missed the joy and freedom we once had together when we shared the goodness of God. I asked if she would mind if Mark came for a visit. He had seen her and needed people like her to visit and encourage the local mums. He said he is *open to change, but please be patient with us.* The Lord started to show her that her lack was in giving, not receiving, for He was always close by for her to receive whatever and whenever she needed. The talk was ended on a positive note, and she is looking forward to Mark's visit. Praise the Lord!

I am tired of Christians building empires to prove their spirituality, Bella, and I will not be goaded into doing any such thing. A

Christian is a dead person with Christ living in him. *Jesus came poor; He lived humble, and He left the same way He came. He built nothing; He wrote nothing, but He gave everything He had.* Where can I find my Jesus? Where can I find my Paul? What do we intend to prove in our buckskin shoes and our swimming pools? To what good is all this to a dead man, may I ask? Who are we kidding? Where is the Spirit of Jesus in this world of tinsel and vain babbling? *"I want to be like Jesus,"* they cry; then turn around and ask for everything that makes them the opposite.

"From Dad, who longs to die, but not to make you cry.
Just knowing that the life that dies, shall live forevermore..."

Sunday, 11 p.m. – June 21st

Had a full day today. After church at St. Gabriel's, I went home and collected all the kids in our street and took them in the mini-bus to the Promenade. The weather was just perfect with thousands of people taking advantage of this unexpected turn of a dismal summer. We had a grand view of the sailboat races on the Mersey River. The Lord topped it off with a spectacular air show at Speke Airport; much like the Blue Angels. You can imagine the delight of the kids to find themselves amidst all this, when half-an-hour before, they were playing in the dirty streets. In the few hours we were together, many of them came and hugged me, they felt so pleased.

Needless to say, the Lord gave me such a blessing of joy. They sang all the way back, and were still singing as they got off the bus. They had tasted a little bit of heaven. Praise my God, for they are His little children.

Went to St. Philemon's evening service, then all the youth piled into the bus and we headed for the tent crusade. I will try to get the Florie boys interested.

Took them to Southport on Friday and it was great. We drove for miles on the beach and they were all over the bus, sitting in the rack on top and hanging on the sides! I even let some of them have a go at driving, and they did very well. We stopped at a restaurant where I was able to witness to the manager, who felt sorry for me taking those kind of youth for a day out! But, I was able to share how much God loved them, and the love He has given me for them. I told him how God touched my heart when I was far worse than they were. The funny part was, I told the boys to bring some of their tapes along, but none of them did. They ended up playing Amy Grant and Dallas Holm the whole day. I was quite happy for small miracles!

(In retrospect, the boys hanging on to and sitting on top of the bus while driving on the beach was not very wise on my part. Thank God no one was injured. I am guilty...again!)

Finished reading 'Intercessor'. Blew my mind. One part of me says, *'go for it,'* the other part of me says, *'put it aside for a while.'* I wonder sometimes, is there any other way but that way? How many of us who think we are on that road to the Heavenly City, end up finding Christian City at the end of it? The best of us seem to cling to life, even though we desire to give our all.

Some answers to your questions, Bella. No, Jim R. didn't give me fatherly advice to go with the check. If he had, he would have gotten it back in the next mail. No, I didn't tell him what I did with it, but I did say I would be held responsible in the sight of God for every penny of it. I can't, for the life of me, understand why he should think my place is with my family, when he feels at liberty to leave his. To those who feel I am here by mistake, I would challenge them to follow me around for a week and see how many youth, who have never trusted an adult in their entire life, have placed a trust in me. Only the people who live here know what kind of miracle that is: it is a direct stamp of God on my life. I can never promise they will come to Christ, that's the Lord's job, but I can say there has never been such a wide open door for them to see the Savior. There will never be a lack of criticism toward the fool that says, *"I'll go."* But the burden is upon the contented who say, *"No."* Amen!

Got a reply back from the Wilkerson Crusade. I would have had to pay three hundred dollars for my training and support for the two weeks. Kind of shocked me, in a way. Where did the simple way go? You know, sleep in classrooms and grab a sandwich on the way out! Well, I can still dream, I guess!

Friday Morning – June 25th

Haven't heard from Kent, as yet. This time of waiting is good for both of us, I'm sure. I have been kept very busy. The lovely Lord is doing marvelous things, constantly keeping me at that state of expectancy, which makes life most interesting. You never know what He's up to, or what He'll do next. Now, having said that, you are probably dying to know what He is doing? I can't explain it in a letter. There are so many little things that make up the whole. I promise to make a tape and have it in the mail by Monday. Promise not to pay any attention to my droning voice. Don't know why, but my voice on a tape bugs me.

Haven't slept much lately. My bedroom window is facing the back street of Mill Street, where a group of young thugs spend entire nights drag racing with stolen cars, then turn them over and burn them. The thing that gets me is, they do it right outside the tenements where they live. Each episode lasts for hours, and not one parent or neighbor even so much as pokes a head out a window. The fear of retaliation is very real. At three this morning, I had had enough, got dressed, and walked to the phone booth. I proceeded to give the police a blow-by-blow on-the-spot report of the hell on the street at that moment. At ninety miles per hour, they just missed another motorist and crashed into the side of the road. The police were there before I even hung up; but, the kids vanished into the tenements.

I went to talk to Sargent Hopwood today (a Christian police officer friend) to see if they want to give me a walkie-talkie, and I'll give them a firsthand description from my window, whenever I see things start to happen. I do want to see them put away, because their actions are vile and mean. I have also prayed that God would loose them from their chains of bondage and darkness to Satan. So, in a way, I should give the Lord a chance to answer those prayers and make myself available, instead of feeling revolted at the sight of them. Gosh, I didn't mean to sound like I hated them. There's no hate in me at all. I would surely love to see them come to Jesus, even at my expense. But, their actions are sickening, and must be brought to a speedy end, before an innocent life is taken away.

Thank you for your prayer in the letter, Bella. I hope you had a letter from me when you got home. You sounded so desperate for one. We both have an insatiable appetite for letters, don't we? How long do you think we can go on like this?

Don't know if I mentioned it before, Bella. I put in for a volunteer probation officer. After being checked out through security, I will have a pass that will enable me to go into prisons and such. I felt impressed to do this, so it may be another open door for ministry. Spent the whole morning (this is now Saturday) moving a Christian couple into a new flat. The Lord gave me such a joy doing it, and even told me not to take a reward for it, even though I've been flat broke for a couple of weeks now. *(used my mini-bus and it's been on empty for ages...thank you, Lord!)* However, I did accept their invite for dinner on Friday. They are a nice young couple, and she will have her first baby in about six weeks.

Remember back a couple of months ago, when I lost two of my best friends, and felt the depths of loneliness for weeks afterward? That was my big test, and I pulled through by leaning on Jesus, once again giving Him my life, such as it is, or was. Then the Lord showed me it was He who pulled everything away so I could feel a little of what He felt on that Cross. I was so glad I never failed Him when the crunch came. Now, I can honestly say I have never been given so many loving friends to enjoy. They are all very precious to me, like God had given each one as a gift.

The morning service will be televised on World in Action. They are doing a special on crime in the inner city about youth. Liverpool 8 has been chosen the worst area in Western Europe for crime and violence. That's quite a statement, isn't it, Bella! If they want to see action, all they have to do is bring a camera up to my room at night and film out my window.

Anyway, it is nice they involve St. Gabriel's in the struggle to change lives in the area. But, they will never capture on film the beauty, love, grace and goodness of our God, because it is shed abroad in a million small ways, seen only by the spiritual eyes of the redeemed.

1 a.m. Sunday Night – Monday Morning

Hi again, Bella,

Couldn't sleep till I praised God with you for His unspeakable joy and goodness to me. I am filled with wonder at what I feel He wants to, and is about to, do. My Sunday started off okay, but I felt kind of down after leaving St. Gabriel's with all the television cameras, and such. I felt everything was done for their benefit, and felt sorry for Jesus. They could never capture Him on camera, and I'm not sure we saw Jesus ourselves.

Anyway, I went home a little heavy, and the weather was cold and windy. I wasn't too keen on taking the children to the promenade like I promised. Many of the kids were waiting for me when I got back, with bottles of lemonade and picnic bags in hand. I told them I wouldn't be going if the weather didn't warm up. I went to my room and laid down, glad to be alone with my headache and ill mood. I hadn't slept much lately with all the goings on each night, and last night was no exception. Someone had gotten married, and the whole neighborhood took on a carnival atmosphere till four a.m., when I finally dozed off.

So, now I felt like sleeping the whole afternoon away. After about an hour, I got to thinking about all those kids and how wonderful it was the Sunday before. I got up very reluctantly and put on my thermal undies, and asked the Lord to give us some sunshine. By the time I got the mini-bus and brought it back, the day had turned into a beautiful afternoon. The squeals of delight from the kids when they saw the bus gave me such joy. I was blessed from my head to my toes.

All the mums and dads watched as the kids hugged me and piled on the bus – all twenty-one of them! I just stood there grinning from ear to ear, as pleased as punch, and I knew that my God reigned in my heart. He is my God forever and has truly made me a child of His. He alone gave me the honor of being the giver of such joy to twenty-one children. I had a little taste of how He must have felt.

One of the Florie boys came by, and seeing me with all those kids, asked me how I was going to manage alone with them. Then he said, *"I'd better go with you."* Bella, he was fantastic with them, and together we had a great time.

There were many touching moments, but the one that touched me the most was a ten year old boy who sat next to me in the park and said, *"I want to thank you, in case nobody else did."* I said it reminded me of the ten lepers Jesus healed, and he said, *"Yes, only one came back to say thank you."* Wow! A little while later he said, *"Can I buy you a Popsicle?"* and I said, *"No thanks, son."* Another kid overheard him and said, *"I'll have it."* and the little boy said, *"I only have enough for one and I wanted it for Frankie."* To think, Bella, I could have stayed in bed and missed all this!

I went to St. Philemon's but left early because I told the Florie boys I would drive by at 7:30 to see if anyone wanted to go to the tent crusade. None of them did. If one had said yes, I'm sure they would all have gone. But pride runs very deep. Anyway, I didn't feel bad because I had done my part, and the rest was up to the Lord.

I have divided my time between both churches, St. Gabriel's and St. Philemon's, and they have both come to love me, and I them. I have never felt comfortable with the Church of England structure of service, but have come to accept it, in order to minister to the youth and the church's outreach to the community, which is excellent. Being around the unchurched so much, I am more aware of the reasons why they won't go. Standing, sitting, reading prayers, using language they don't understand, a feeling that the church people are too far out of their class, etc. St. Gabriel's is considering me for full-time ministry of visitation. That would mean complete loyalty to them and the church structure, and I'm not sure I can do that.

The 468 Boys Club has a full-time position they would like to offer me, but they are afraid my Christian commitment is too strong. But one thing emerges out of all this. There is a definite love bond between us (churches and youth clubs) and they trust and admire me for my total commitment to the work I have been called to do.

Frank and his mates from the 468 club

I think I'll go make myself a cup of tea and toast, I'm starving! Gave Mr. Little a ride home from the crusade, and he insisted on giving me fifty pence. Now I can buy a stamp for this letter; otherwise, it will get longer each day.

I'm teaching Danny, one of the 468 Club boys, how to play guitar. We spend quite a bit of time together. He said to me today, *"The last few times I went to the pub, I didn't enjoy it like I used to."* He has been to a few after-church meetings with me, along with another youth named Fred. You are going to hear a lot about Fred in the future. He's the tough guy who wrote the song about the little baby inside the mother who is having an abortion. He is halfway through writing a song about a guy who gave up everything to come to Liverpool to tell everybody about Jesus. I can't believe this guy. The three of us were visiting in my room. As they got up to go, he said, *"Frank, why don't you pray for me and Danny before we go."* I couldn't believe he said that. Anyway, after I prayed, he prayed too! Listen to the way he prayed, Bella.

"God, if you're up there, la, then show me, la, so I'll know what to do, you know what I mean, la? I know I'm bad, but you've gotta show me so I can understand."

Note: *Fred went on to become a Church of England Pastor, and is still serving the Lord till this day, over thirty years later. Obviously, God answered such a wonderful prayer of the heart, and "showed him, la."*

Fred is full of surprises, and as much of a Nicky Cruz as I've ever seen. His mom told me he said I was a 'boss guy.' That's pretty heavy stuff from him. His girlfriend of three years up and left him, and he came to me for help. At one of the youth meetings he fell for a Christian girl and said to the boys at the club, *"She's the first girl I ever met who I didn't want to have sex with, she was different."* All the guys roared with laughter, because this just wasn't like Fred. The only thing he could say was, *"You dummies could never understand that."* Neither could Fred.

Newsflash! *The Bishop of Guildford told the Press that, although Jesus Christ had been the way to God for him, he nonetheless believed that there is "a real experience of God in other religions." He added, "The view that other religions worship a false God would be alien to this committee."*

Wow! To think a Bishop would call Jesus a liar is beyond me! The committee should be disbanded immediately, and the Bishop locked up in a windowless room with only a Bible to read. In John 14:6, Jesus said, *"I am the way, the truth, and the life.* ***No one*** *comes to the Father except through me."*

Again, in John 3:16-18, Jesus said, *"For God so loved the world that He gave His only begotten Son, that whoever believes in* ***Him*** *should not perish but have everlasting life. For God did not send His Son into the world to condemn the world, but that the world* ***through Him*** *might be saved. He who believes in* ***Him*** *is not condemned; but he who does not believe is condemned already, because he has not believed in the name of the only begotten Son of God."*

When Jesus was praying in the garden just before His crucifixion, He fell on His face and prayed, *"O My Father, if it is possible, let this cup pass from Me; nevertheless, not what I will, but what You will." Matt. 26:39*

Here, Jesus is clearly asking if His Father could find ***another way*** and the answer was clearly, 'No.' It could only be accomplished with a ***perfect*** sacrifice, and Jesus, the Son of God, was the only perfect one.

In Acts 4:12, the Word of God says, *"Nor is there salvation in any other, for there is no other name under heaven given among men by which we must be saved."*

In I Timothy 2:5, the apostle Paul tells Timothy, *"For there is one God and one Mediator between God and men, the Man Christ Jesus."*

I could go on and on, but I think I've made the point. If you are going to be a minister of God, you need to know what it is that God wants you to say about Him. Otherwise, you make His Word of no effect.

Oh, I'm dying to give another example, and so I will, just so people like our reverend Bishop can squirm a little.

In Galatians 1:6-10, Paul says, *"I marvel that you are turning away so soon from Him who called you in the grace of Christ, to a different gospel. Which is not another: but there are some who trouble you and want to pervert the gospel of Christ. But even if we, or an angel from heaven, preach any other gospel to you than what we have preached to you, let him be accursed. As we have said before, so now I say again, if anyone preaches any other gospel to you than what you have received, let him be accursed. For do I now persuade men, or God? Or do I seek to please men? For if I still pleased men, I would not be a bond-servant of Christ."*

Friday Night – July 3rd

"Be of good cheer, I have overcome the world." - Jesus
"Jesus is Lord of all the earth." - God
"The King is coming, hallelujah! In all His Glory, hallelujah!" - His children

My dear sweet wife,

How have I managed five months without you? It is nothing short of a miracle, I assure you! You are forever on my mind, and my love for you has grown so deep, I would give anything just to reach out and touch you. Only God, in His infinite wisdom could have foreseen the kind of woman I would need in such times as these; for I have not offered you the normal life. Who but you could stand so fast in faith that God is in this with me. May He honor you, as He has so many times in days gone by, as being worthy to sit at His feet and enjoy the fullness of His love.

Just got back from dinner with the couple I helped move last week. She is eight months pregnant, and what a sweetheart. Poor girl, she made me guest of honor and invited a few friends, then discovered her stove wouldn't work. There was a last minute dash to get something on the table, but I enjoyed every minute of it.

Brought my guitar, but after dinner, the guests started playing Beatles records and started dancing. I called Robin in the kitchen and told her I was going to slip out quietly, because I didn't feel this was pleasing to God. She had tears in her eyes, but I assured her of my love and friendship. I promised to come back soon for a quiet evening of worship and singing praises to God.

All is well, but my heart aches for these Christians here. They hunger for more of God, yet find no harm in listening and dancing to the world's music. They have never been challenged to forsake the world's ways, so they dabble in a little bit of everything, then wonder why the world isn't impressed with their testimony. Most of all, why they don't have power to live the life God has for them.

Only by the grace of God has my testimony held true; for Christians are starting to ask questions and inquire about this strange creature who has shown up in their midst. Why does he pray like that? Is he paid by anyone? The questions are endless, but the answer Mark likes to give most is, *"He is a man who has taken God at His Word."*

Bella, I had a great meeting with Mark and David, the assistant pastor, today, and guess what David said to me. *"Frank, till you came, I felt fine; now I am not so sure. You have made me re-evaluate myself, because you have shown me a more excellent way. I am hungry again!"*

You don't know what real humility is till someone says something like that to you, and you honestly feel you are nothing more than the biggest stinker around. They see me one way, and I see me another. But, God has given me a supernatural desire to lift Him up high and proclaim His greatness; even though I may be struggling myself. It is like He has made up His mind to use me *in spite of myself.* I am enjoying the fruit of His blessing, no matter what!

Danny, Fred, and I have become inseparable, even though they are not yet Christians. They want to help me in my work for the Lord. I have to laugh at the whole silly idea, yet it is such a beautiful thing to experience. In dead earnest, they asked me today, *"Do you think your wife will like us?"* Bella, you wouldn't think it, but these are two tough guys. I told them they are getting soft on me, and we had a good laugh. They bought me lunch, then made me drive to the park. They had me share Jesus with them for about an hour. I can't believe God is so good to me. If I could get ahold of Him, I would hug Him!

We three, along with a dozen boys from the 468 Club, will take off for a weekend camping trip in Wales. Then, right after that, a week's retreat with Reg Ash and needy families from the area. Then, three days later, a week's camp with the Florie boys. So, instead of trying to write a letter, I will just keep a daily diary for you and send it each week.

My only purpose in all this activity is to see God move in a mighty way, so that these boys will remember this season for a different reason than those gone before. My only prayer is that I will find time to seek God and His will at all times; never to be caught up with all the goings on, but be in tune to move when the Lord says to. That is easier said than done, but I must do it.

> ***God,*** *we expect your greatness to be manifest*
> *in the strangest places, at the strangest times,*
> *so make me aware at all times. Amen.*

Part of my talk with Mark today was on the need for a church or fellowship that catered to the needs of the people who could not feel at home in a structured church. I am meeting more and more people who feel this way. They are simple people. *"Blessed are the poor in spirit, for they shall be comforted."* Through God's grace and mercy, I have come to identify with them. I have come to love them, and will not rest till I find a way for them to find peace with God. And find a living faith in Jesus Christ our Lord and Savior, who gave Himself for these very people, who we have rejected for so long. May God establish right now, His will for their needs to be met.

> ***God,*** *set your seal upon me by giving me one hundred souls to love for you. Give me a burning desire that will never go out, then a mighty move of your Holy Spirit to capture my heart, soul and spirit for the work ahead. I am believing that You want to save them. I look forward to the fruit and the workers to harvest the field with me. The bond of love will be like none since the early church. You can do it!*

Morning

No letter! Oh well, never mind. I will look forward to lots of good reading when I get back. Thought I would hear from Kent by now. My only hope is he isn't struggling, but resting in the love of Jesus. If he needs time to establish himself through his church, I would feel it was God's will at this time. For God is perfect in all His ways, and we are but servants to rejoice and obey.

Bella, if I thought for one moment this wasn't worth the sacrifice you and the family are making, I would be home in a second. Be assured, there is nothing more certain in the whole world. Rejoice with me for a little while longer; for God is a rewarder, and our joy will be full. Praise God!

I must come to a close, but not before I tell you I am full of love for you all. My hand is shaking, as God's love fills me with excitement and anticipation for the days ahead. Is this any way to live? You bet it is! *"Blessed are they who hunger and thirst after righteousness, for they shall be filled."*

"Rejoice, my children; for in Me you have everything." - Jesus

Tuesday Afternoon – July 7th

Hello, my sweet Bella,

This is going to be a hard letter to write. So many things have been happening, it's hard to keep up with it. The weekend camping trip for the 468 boys comprised of one bus leaving early Saturday, and my bus leaving the same afternoon. The Florie boys got wind of it and begged me to take them along. It was a beautiful, hot summer's day and I felt kind of sorry for them, so I squeezed eight of them in with the promise that they wouldn't let me down, and try to get along with the 468 boys.

On the way, we stopped at a cafe' where the Florie boys proceeded to molest a teenage girl in the back room, and rob all the money from an ice cream truck. Fred told me this much later, as I was unaware of it all. Danny told me the boys had also robbed the chippy in the village we had stopped at.

At one point I took the guitar to sing around the campfire to get everybody involved, but gave up after a while, they were so rowdy. Danny, Fred and I went back to our tent. Before bedding down, they asked me to pray; then Fred prayed, then Danny, then Fred again, then Danny, then Fred gave his heart to the Lord, and couldn't quit praying for half an hour! He thanked God many times for me. I just lay there with my eyes closed and marveled at the crazy way God chooses to do things. Outside, it sounded like hell had broken loose, but in our little tent, heaven had come down.

After only two hours sleep, the youth leader opened my tent and told me to get those Florie boys out of his sight! So, at 5 a.m. we were on our way home again, minus two windows in my mini-bus, and damage to a brand new tent. I said not one word all the way back. I know my silence said it all, as one by one they told me they were sorry. Now I feel I must take a different approach. There is a strong possibility I won't take them on that week's camp-out on the 17th.

Toxteth Riots

Sunday night, riots broke out. In an instant my world exploded. Chaos reigned everywhere. Like a bad dream, the unthinkable began to unfold all around me. I stood transfixed and helpless in the very epicenter of the Toxteth riots; Northumberland Street and Park Road. This was the very community that I'd grown up in. It was beginning to look more like a war zone than my childhood neighborhood.

Toxteth Riots

A police jeep screeched to a halt in the middle of Park Road. The rioters pulled back and melted into the crowds of onlookers lining each side of the street. For a long moment, a strange silence fell over the scene. The crackling sounds of storefronts burning could now be heard, along with the distant sounds of many sirens. Smoke darkened the already gray sky. A rock bounced off the side of the police jeep, then another. The window of the jeep rolled down, then quickly back up, as rocks began to rain down on the vehicle. It sped away.

I watched in horror as men, women and children, now freed from all restraints and pretense, converged on the burning stores, smashing doors and windows. Like colonies of ants, they streaked in and out of the buildings carrying armloads of goods. Clothing, shoes and electronics soon littered the street, as people, though loaded down, still fought over each item that had dropped on the ground. My skin crawled. I had never felt *evil* before.

"I'd be right in there with them if you hadn't come," I heard Fred say. I looked at him standing beside me, then Danny on my other side, who nodded in solemn agreement. In voicing gratitude for their changed hearts, they had reminded me that, even in the midst of such darkness, there was hope.

I got up early the next morning and went out to see the carnage the riots had left behind. All the little shops that had been there forever were now reduced to piles of smoldering ashes. But it wasn't over. Word spread quickly that rioters from as far away as London and Birmingham were now making their way to Liverpool to join in the fight.

On every street corner police made their presence known. Others walked through the neighborhood talking to anyone who was willing to engage in conversation. Some women, bless their hearts, came out of their houses and offered the 'Bobbies' cups of tea and biscuits. But as night fell, the air took on that foreboding that I'd felt the night before. I knew it was going to be another long night.

Park Road was again filling up with people in what seemed like a mood of morbid festivity. In the distance a faint sound of thunder could be heard. The steady beat of thunder grew louder. Soon, row after row of uniformed police came into view, night sticks beating against their riot shields. Rocks flew through the air. An officer fell under the barrage, then another, but they kept on coming. The rioters backed up, then dispersed down the side streets, only to regroup behind the police.

The police turned in unison and began the steady march back in the other direction. Burning buildings began to light up the night sky again. I witnessed a number of police falling under the continued barrage of rocks. I looked at a young boy nearest to me and said, *"What do you think you're going to do with that rock? Put it down!"* He seemed to look right through me. I felt this empty feeling, like he, along with all the rest, had stepped into a world I could not enter. They were no longer just boys and girls, but possessed beings, incapable of emotion.

Trouble began to flare up in every direction, as store after store was set on fire. I stood opposite C&C as dozens of youth swarmed inside. Lines of police, not twenty yards away, marched slowly in the opposite direction. They could not turn around because they were facing a mob raining rocks upon them. The buildings burnt out of control as fire engines were fighting fires elsewhere.

I decided it was all too much for me. I had to leave to be with Susan and the kids. I felt a deep sadness. By the time it was all over, four hundred and fifty police were injured. Five hundred rioters were arrested and over seventy buildings destroyed. To my mind, it was the natural result of a society that had long ago turned its back on God.

Tuesday, Midnight

Things seem to be settling down somewhat. Police are all over the place keeping the youth on the move, not allowing them to form into groups. Fred and I walked around for a few hours talking to many of the police who were very friendly and grateful for a little chat. Early on, we had both gone to a prayer meeting. We came away feeling like the Lord had a restraining hand on things. Fred gave his testimony too, and it was great.

Morning

Bella! What a glorious letter. So full of victory! When I put it down I was so full of love and praise for Jesus. I just put up my hands and blessed His Holy Name! I feel we are in the stream of living water and I want to drown. Can you sense the Victory!? My spirit was so full, I composed a letter in my head to the biggest fool of all time, Satan.

By the time I had walked to my favorite cuppa downtown, I was crying with joy. Your letter was so full of things to thank God for and so full of things to pray for, that I will be kept busy with prayerful joy for a long time to come. You are my exquisite gem and I love you.

It is a beautiful morning with the sun shining. I long to hold my two girls' hands and walk forever. This is my suffering right now. *"But the suffering of this present time is nothing compared to the joy that awaits us."* So, be of good cheer, my lovely girls, for our Heavenly Father can see our aching hearts and He will bind up the brokenhearted. For I trust Him.

Monday, Noon – July 13th (New Brighton)

Went out to get the mini-bus this morning. Who do you think drives by and waves to me not ten feet away? *Margaret Thatcher*! She slipped into town unannounced. The hate for her runs very deep in these parts. She came to see first-hand the destruction of the last weeks' riots. May God use this death of a city to bring new life for His Name's sake.

I delivered a letter to the Daily Echo this morning for "Letters to the Editor." I hope if they print it at all, they don't decide to put it in the religious section. Oh well, I'll just have to leave that up to the Lord. Sometimes I get to feeling so inadequate with flashes of inspiration that fizzle all too soon. I want to be a Paul, yet I find myself tripped by the simplest things. Death of self must be the hardest to achieve, yet it's the most basic thing to full power in the Lord.

I took eighteen kids out yesterday. It was truly a sacrifice. I wanted so bad just to be alone and rest. Guess what those little stinkers did! They collected money from each other and presented a whole handful of change to me as a gift. I told them the trips were absolutely free, and I would not accept the money. They all, with one voice shouted, *"We want you to have it!"* I could hardly hold back from crying. One kid brought me a package of cookies from his mum, *"special for Frankie."* Another kid gave me an envelope with two pounds in it addressed, *"For Frankie's sandwich."* Most said their mum packed extra in their lunch to share with me. One dad came up and gave me a pound. I told him that this was all getting out of hand, as it was meant to be free. As our eyes met I got the feeling we understood each other as he pressed the pound into my hand.

It is at times like these that I want to leave my body behind and soar into the unknown, only to find my wings are clipped, and I can't leave the ground.

I think of you all the time and wish we could be together, yet the obstacles are many and the way not yet clear. Now I must trust in the Lord, for I can't see my way out of the dilemma. *"Hold fast to the promise that He alone knows our needs, and will give us the desire of our hearts in due time."*

Thursday the 15th

My sweet Bella,

What a sad looking little girl on the card you sent. Makes me want to just rush on home and comfort you, never to leave you again. You are the sweetest, bravest, most tender woman I have ever known.

When Jesus fell under the weight of His cross, I wanted Him to get up and keep going, refusing the help of Simon of Cyrene; after all, Charlton Heston would have done no less, and I wanted to be proud of Him, too.

Bless you and Jesus, Bella, and anybody else whose cross is too heavy to bear. His tender body was no different than yours or mine. If Jesus allowed Simon to ease the pain, could I do any less to ease yours, my love? His humanity was displayed for all the world to see. I love Him even more!

Together, like Jesus and Simon, we too can reach the top of the hill. There was no shame for Him, neither will there be for you. You are my tender wife and family. I am ready to leave at this present time, to be with you. I have no means right now, but will await your direction. Meanwhile, I'll make all things in order, ready to leave at the shortest possible notice.

Seeing as I only wrote you two days ago, this one will be short. I spent all day yesterday in my room. Seems like I need to be alone to write. I have written, but not finished, an 'allegory' of England, as I see it. How it will end I'm not sure, but it has been interesting doing it.

I believe the riots are only the tip of the iceberg. If God doesn't intervene in this country's affairs, I'm afraid there is no hope. I have come to get a clearer picture and deeper insight to how deep the problem is. I can say with conviction, there is no way out of their dilemma. The country is on the brink of virtual collapse. A miracle is the only thing we can hope for.

The Christians of the world should be praying day and night for this country, for if it falls, great is the fall of it. The world itself will not recover from it.

God is perfect in all His ways, and who can fathom the riches of His love and grace. The world has yet to see the wonders of His hand. *"With a word from Him the world was formed." "With a word from Him the world was saved!"*

Sunday the 19th

What a day I've had. Twenty-four kids. We went to Ainsdale beach for the day and it was very windy and rainy. All the kids got mucked in anyway, some swimming fully clothed, others falling in fully clothed. Ugh. What a mess, but they seemed to have a good time of it.

My gas tank was on empty for the whole trip back, and I was sure praying up a storm. It was nothing short of a miracle that we made it back. So, now I am just resting. Beginning to tell my age.

I expect Fred and Danny to drop by any minute now. Can you believe it? They went to church tonight and I stayed home! Last night we three had a Bible study lasting four hours, singing and praying up a storm. It was on the Second Coming of Jesus. Afterward, Fred told Danny to accept Jesus into his life, otherwise we'd be going without him, and we sure wanted him with us!

Danny told Fred not to get too pushy, he'd come in his own good time! We have become inseparable, and Danny does pray, sing and go to church right along with us. So, it is just a matter of time. Fred wants the baptism of the Holy Spirit and was very disappointed when I prayed and he didn't get it. Still, he went home and threw everything out that would be a hindrance in his walk and full commitment to Jesus.

At first, he fought me on my hard stand of all or nothing; now he is glad and wants to become the best. He sees what the moderate Christian life looks like. He is constantly challenging their ideals. I have told him to quit it, till he grows in wisdom and knowledge; otherwise, he will sound and look like a young fool, even though the things he says are very good.

Ever since my decision to visit you for a while, I have had total peace about it. Now, I can't think about anything else! Praise God for His love and caring for you; that He could get through to me in such a beautiful way. I had no inkling that this was going to happen, but I can sure see how He set me up for it. You and your '*lonesome little card*'. Now, the time is going so slow, and I'm busting to get to you and the kids.

Well, the two lads came by and it's now midnight. I want to get this off in the mail tomorrow, so I'll keep going. The lads enjoyed the service, and Fred was asked to share his testimony at a future date. He said he didn't think he would. I told him to check with his Boss before turning anything down. His will must always come first. I think he got the message.

I'm going home! Praise the Lord!

Got up very late. The last thing I remember is squeezing the clock to death to make it quit. It's overcast today. Very light drizzle. Just perfect for walking. Don't know why I'm writing, I don't have a thing to say. I must quit mooning about you.

God's Word is so good. If love was not its greatest aim, I would throw it away! But, it is full of love, love, love.

Exhortation

> ***Oh, foolish man. You search forever for the secret to life: love, joy, and peace. It is all within reach of a bended knee and a humble heart. You refuse it because you are proud and arrogant. It doesn't meet your concept of a man. And you'd go through hell before you would bow to the very God who made you. Vanity, all is vanity. It blows away in the wind, gone forever. Your nakedness and wretchedness will someday be revealed for all to see. You will wonder at the price you paid for vanity...***

Tuesday, 7:30 September 8th

Hello, Bella,

Miss you sooo much, you little sweetheart. It's taken me till now to settle down to a semblance of a routine. The flight was very good, but I didn't get any sleep. Guess what? No clammy hands! Could it be I am getting used to flying? The train from London was held up just outside of Liverpool for over an hour. Some poor kid touched the overhead wires and was killed.

Haven't done much. Sleeping on and off at odd hours. All the family seem in good spirits. I got lots of hugs and kisses from Susan's three kids and they were made up with their little slippers. No one expected me to come back, but Susan kept my room just as it was, 'just in case.'

The mini-bus looks awful. Seems like the Florie had it parked outside the club when a stolen car, driven by a thirteen year old ran smack into it. The youth leader is going to get it fixed as best he can, but I doubt it will ever be the same.

Reg Ash, the Florie manager, was pleased as punch to see me back. That guy really likes me. I told him I was interested in a full-time paying job at the 468 club. He pleaded with me to wait a little longer. He wants to make room for me at the Florie. Praise the Lord! The boys were genuinely pleased to see me and chatted excitedly the whole time. Couldn't help thinking, the groundwork has been laid; now for the building.

My Dear One,

Sorry I haven't written but one letter. I'm finding it very difficult this time to settle into some kind of a routine. Three days after I got back, I was off for a week with the 468 club on this caving venture. It was a very rewarding experience, but very demanding on the body.

There's a house/shop on Mill Street I've been interested in for 3,500 pounds (about 7,000 dollars). Needs lots of work, but I do feel it could be a great beginning. I was fortunate to sell the mini-bus for 275 pounds. Only lost 25 pounds, so I don't feel bad. I did get a lot of use out of it, and it did look awful bad from the accident I told you about.

I do long to get back to a more spiritual awareness, but have not, as yet, had much chance. I don't want to get caught up in the activities and miss the most important thing. Salvation! For now, I am building that foundation of trust and having fantastic results. Pray that my popularity will not mean a compromise for them or for me...*Dream a dream, see a vision, and God will bring it to pass...*

My dearest Bella,

Thank you for a wonderful letter. It never fails to bring me joy to see it sitting on the hallway floor, when I go down to make tea and toast. The tea always tastes better at those times, as I snuggle back into bed to read it.

Every bone in my body aches. We went pot-holing on Thursday in Derbyshire. I thought it was like caving, so didn't I get a big surprise! We entered by a hole in the ground, no bigger than a man-hole, with water pouring in on top of us. Right away we were drenched. For four hours, we squeezed, knelt, and squirmed our way through passages a rat wouldn't care to go. We had two 25-foot drops on a rope ladder, with waterfalls cascading on top of us. We crawled around with our caving suits and 'wellies' (boots) full of water.

Caving Adventure

At one point, my claustrophobia was so bad, I was a right mess. I just prayed and sang up a storm to the Lord, and it passed! I was able to go on without anyone being the wiser, and I never got the feeling back. I even encouraged three would-be dropouts to continue, and was one of a few who would climb the ladder up a waterfall. There was no way you could climb it by sight; the water covered you the whole time. We were all happy when it was over and emerged into the bright afternoon sunshine.

Those experiences never fail to bring us closer together, and the feeling of accomplishment was great. The next day, Friday, your husband took a group to Ainsdale, and did most of the sand-surfing at speeds up to forty miles an hour. I had sand ground in places I dare not mention, and came home looking like a rag doll, but happy! This morning I am paying the price of a 42 year old acting like a teenager.

Midnight

Had a chat with Mark. He wants me to be a counselor for the Nicky Cruz Crusade, which, of course, is great with me. Don't feel quite as excited about it as I should, but guess that stems from the tremendous letdown I felt at his last one. Still, we must believe God for a miracle.

The big news over here is the sending of forty warships to Argentina to recapture the Falklands. I see it as a game of pride. Many good lives may be lost because of it.

Man has come a long way down the road to nowhere. It is hard to find human kindness any more. Selfishness, greed, pride, and a spirit of contention fills the world, and never more so than in England. I will write a book someday on what I have seen and felt since coming here. No one will like it, but it will be the absolute truth. God's hand of mercy is England's only hope. At this moment, I think they would sooner spit in His face than acknowledge their desperate need of Him. I'd better quit that kind of talk before I depress you, Bella.

This will cheer you up. *Prince Charles* waved at me on Thursday. I never knew he was in town. I thought to myself, *"What a strange life I have here! I walk out the door last September and the Prime Minister, Margaret Thatcher, waves at me. I get a flat tire on my bike and turn around to find Charles, the Prince of Wales, waving at me!"* But, it's all commonplace when you realize the King of all creation lives in me! Now that's exciting!

Sunday Night

Just re-read your last letter and I don't like it when you're sad. It's at these times that I get the greatest urge to throw in the towel and go home and live a normal life. I sometimes feel guilty that you've been cheated out of a normal life, Bella. You demand so very little and deserve so much more. Yet, I find I am giving my all to a people who are so unbending; who demand so much and give so little. But, we must leave it in God's hands to be the final Judge of it all.

I sometimes wonder if you think I'm enjoying this life, Bella; what with all the activities and such. With all my heart I can say, no! My joy comes from the realization that I am capable of going through it all, when I never thought I could. I have learned to survive and go far beyond my known capabilities, thanks to my Lord, who gives me what I need. Too long have these people taken the viewpoint that a Christian has lost all reality with life.

But, can you blame them for thinking that? We should, as Christians, be more involved with life than anybody! I'm not talking about enjoying things for enjoyment's sake, so much as being involved that we may have better opportunity to influence them. They are not impressed that we go to church or have Bible studies. They are not even impressed that we don't go to pubs, get into fights or curse every other word.

What does impress them is a life that is involved with them. A life that shares love, peace, and encouragement, when theirs is filled with bitterness and hate. Their constant complaints of society's harsh treatment to them falls limp when I'm around, for I have taken away their defense. They received and demanded more. I had nothing, asked for nothing, and filled my time with serving others. I took a job that most men would refuse because it didn't pay enough to live. I am able to give extra for my keep, buy the things I need, and still give as I find the need. No one can ever say, *"But, my situation is different."*

I have lived and experienced them all and they are without excuse. Jesus is the answer for every situation and they have living proof. Satan loves to get me when I'm down with *"You are wasting your time here. You're not saving souls."* I look around and have to admit I'm not saving many souls, and feel a little more depressed. Then the Lord hits me with the truth, and the father of lies has to slink back into his grubby little hole.

"Ye shall be witnesses of Me." And that's exactly what I am. I am a witness to God's saving grace. *"One sows, another waters, and God gives the increase."* I've got a good feeling that my job is *witnessing, sowing and watering.*

Well, Bella Rossiter, you have one crazy husband. The longer I'm over here, the stranger my letters get. Hope you don't mind me going on a bit like I do. If I have any more in the morning, I will add; otherwise, I will say goodbye and I love you all so much. Please be happy! Take a step back and see it from where God is standing. We have everything when we have Christ. Think deeply on what that really means, and when it hits you, you can't help but sing for joy!

Thank you, Bella, for your kindness, patience, long-suffering, love and gentleness toward me.

September 29, 1981, Evening

My dearest sweet Bella,

Your letter was delicious (highly pleasing to the taste), according to Webster, and Deb's card was a delight (provided great pleasure). So, you can see I'm using my new dictionary to best advantage. I looked up 'supreme love' because that's how I felt, and this is what it said: *highest, final feeling of deep affection.*

A funny thing happened to me just now, Bella. While I was writing to you, I heard an awful racket outside my window. When I looked out I saw all these kids banging and playing on these beautiful looking musical instruments. I recognized most of the kids and knew they had broken into some place and would destroy them if I didn't do something fast. I went downstairs and told Susan I was going out to persuade the kids to give them to me. As I approached, they all ran away except one, so I told him I would be willing to buy them back and not give the police any names when I took the stuff to the police station. With much persuasion and about five pounds, I was able to get most of them back to Susan's and even got the kids to help me find some of the pieces strewn around the street.

While we were doing this, the police arrived and I told them I had most of the things upstairs and whoever owned them owes me a fiver. I got the shock of my life, Bella. He said I broke the law by paying for it and may have to charge me for possession of stolen goods. I had to laugh because it sounded so funny, but he wasn't kidding!

Just then, Pastor Mark came by and I called him over and told him the story. Mark turned to the police and said, *"I vouch for this man's integrity."* The cop said I still broke the law and his superior may send him back for me. I've got the giggles, Bella, just thinking about it and tomorrow's headlines. I may have to finish this in jail! Tee-hee, as Deb would say. Can you imagine the look on the face of Sergeant Hopwood (a personal friend) when he opens the door to serve breakfast and finds me grinning back at him? Oh, I would gladly spend tonight in jail just to see that!

Went to the football game yesterday to see Liverpool play. Could have thought of better things to do with my time but toward noon, I felt freedom to go. It was with Fred, Danny and a couple of other guys from the 468 boys club and there were times for witness. The people at the game were very profane and uncouth in every way, even going to the toilet where they stood. The boys were aware of it because I was with them and I didn't have to say a word.

Thank you for the 'three precious things' in regard to me. Love is blind!

Saw a shop and living quarters for sale on Mill Street which was in total disrepair, but which had lots of possibilities. I told the boys at the Florie about it and they would be willing to get stuck in with me and fix it up. I could see myself making a big pot of stew or soup and sandwiches each day, as we all worked together to make this into a beautiful place for Christian outreach. That's all some of these kids need is a challenge and they could be great.

Anyway, I had the vision, so off I went to the owner. I told him about the work I was doing with the youth and asked him to give me the place for free and he ended up throwing me out. I went home and wrote him a letter, of which I will send you a copy. I felt the man was not open to spiritual things so I avoided that area and worked on that which he would relate to. I'll let you know the outcome in my next letter.

September 20, 1981

Dear Mr. Linford,

After talking with you I felt I had not touched you, the man. Being in business for so long, you naturally see all transactions in business terms, but this was not the kind of appeal I came to make. In a world full of "What do I get out of it," I have learnt the secret of life: "It is more blessed to give than to receive."

I find I have nothing to give but myself, so I set out to give it, leaving my lovely wife, children, home, job and friends in hopes that I could be of help to the people of Toxteth, mainly the youth.

I have succeeded to a degree, in winning their trust and respect, which is no small miracle in this day and age. Therefore, I now find them listening and acting upon much that I have to say. I want to influence them away from the common belief that government is there for the sole purpose of meeting all their needs and blaming government for all the ills and hard times. Also, when businesses succeed, it's not necessarily through exploiting the poor but in most cases it's through plain hard work and much sacrifice.

Since coming here I have met much apathy and very little faith in man and the future. I need people like you to restore my sagging confidence, for I too, am not immune to the feelings of despair, if that is all I encounter.

Could you find it in yourself to trust someone like me with a gift? To you, the property means a couple of thousand pounds. To me, it would be a gift of love that could spark me into new and exciting adventures with the people of this community.

When I mentioned to a young friend the possibility of acquiring your property free of charge, he had only one comment, "Fat chance, you're just dreaming!" Is the time for dreams over forever, Mr. Linford? Personally, I don't think so.

If the above is not possible, I would be interested in the minimum you would require for the property. I have no funds at this time but would do all in my power to obtain it. I am ready to move on it as soon as possible, so your cooperation will be much appreciated. Thank you.

Yours truly, Frank Rossiter

P.S. Looks like the police don't want me. They allowed me to take the musical instruments back to the very grateful St. Malachey's girls' school. However, I didn't have the heart to tell them they owed me a 'fiver!'

Saturday, Noon – September 26th

My dearest Bella,

Thank you for your beautiful letter. The feeling I get when I see it lying there on the hall floor is pure delight. I think it must be love, don't you? Getting up this morning was a little difficult. It looked rainy and dismal out there, plus I have a bad cold again. I decided to come downtown and write you a nice letter, and then call you on the phone just to hear your sweet voice. Right now, it's only four in the morning, your time. I can see you all snug and sleeping, and you don't know yet I'm going to call.

Had no reply from the shop owner as yet, but I did make a seed faith offering. I had lunch with a Christian couple last week who shared how they had been praying to God for a need they had. Unknown to them, I had the answer in my pocket. Two hundred and fifty pounds from the sale of the mini-bus. They said they would pray about it when I offered it to them. Three days later they said, *Yes, they believe it was the Lord!"* By this time I had forgotten my offer and had looked at the money as a down payment for the Mill Street property. With a smile on my face and very heavy feet, I dropped it in their mail box. I was broke again; but then, have I ever been able to hold on to money? I perceive, if I need something, it has to be through the hand of God; and what better way to receive. I am no authority on faith, and it comes no easier to me than any other; but I must go on believing that what is loss for me now, will turn to gain sometime in the future.

A boyhood friend is dying with cancer. I used to watch him out of my bedroom window, walking his daily trek to the betting shop after each race. One day I got to talking to him about Jesus. He had to acknowledge the miracle in my life; on walking away he shouted over his shoulder, *"It's too late for me, Frank,"* at which I shouted back, *"It's never too late, Vern!"* Two months ago, on missing seeing his familiar figure, I inquired and found out he was sick. I went to see him. There wasn't an opening to share much with him, but he was grateful for the visit. Last week I heard he was dying, so I dropped by again and found him very thin and bedridden. He was in constant pain now and I knew it was only a matter of weeks. Still, he left no room for me to share. I knew I had to make the break while I still had time, so I asked him if he believed in miracles and he said yes. *"Then I'm going to pray for one,"* I told him. I prayed a beautiful prayer of God raising him up so all can see the love that God has for them all. I want to see him healed, Bella, more than anything in the world. Sometimes I wish I was a holy man like Paul, and had authority over such suffering, but I feel so inadequate to the task. I am so human it makes me sick. In order to fast and pray like my heart knows I should, I feel I have to literally force my body into responding an inch at a time. Then I give up so easily and ask God to work without me. I don't want Him to wait for me to be ready, otherwise, nothing will get done. So, I'm here and I wonder how He ever got me this far!

Evening

After talking to you this afternoon, I walked out into a downpour of rain and got soaked through, so I went home and took a nice hot bath. It was good hearing your voice again. I hope it was worth it to you. I promise to wait till I can't stand it any longer before calling again.

Not sure if I should let some of our Christian friends know my need for the shop on Mill Street. After saying that, I feel I should just leave it all in the Lord's hands, unless He shows me otherwise.

The stock market is dropping with leaps and bounds this past week, Bella. The worse since the war. Lots of intelligent people are very concerned at this present time. I see it as such a godless country and very sick in mind, soul and body. If God has taken His hand away then nothing but total collapse is well in sight. I know that's a grim observation, but one I didn't come to lightly.

Those musical instruments I saved were stolen again the very next night. I am one of the very few adults who are not openly cursed and abused by the youth. I could write for literally days on the total breakdown of every area of life, but I mustn't, for I must drag my eyes back to Jesus, who alone brings sanity and meaning into such a meaningless society.

Sorry to say, I don't look forward to church in the morning. Everything seems so lifeless and dry. I keep thinking, *"If only I, or someone, could be so full of Jesus and move among these people with love and power and anointing of God, and change and set these people on fire!"* My heart wants to be the one, but my body won't respond. One day soon, I feel I'll go all the way or leave for good. Nothing short of total commitment to the will of God will ever be effective here. None of our training in evangelism, Bible studies, prayer meetings, church services or anything else I have ever encountered, will turn the tide of sickness engulfing our world today – except men full of the Holy Ghost with power over all the demons of hell. We need to shake the world with the glory of God, but first we must shake the world out of ourselves. Sometimes I fall asleep thinking maybe tomorrow, only to wake up feeling just as weak as I did the day before. I want to be flowing in God's grace, but I want to wake up with it and not earn it or suffer for it...

Don't mind me, Bella. I'm just writing down some thoughts. I should have ended this letter hours ago, but sometimes I get carried away. If I don't have any more to say in the morning, I'll send it off. So good night, love. Thanks for all you have been to me. My last thoughts of the day are of you and your steadfastness.

Sunday Afternoon

Church was boring, but I love these people and they me. Not sure I want to go back, but I do want to have fellowship with them. I know we all need each other. But to be subject to that service week after week, I'm not sure of. This week I need to step out boldly on some things I've been contemplating doing. I know I'm going to look like a fool, but I get tired of playing the game. Popularity can become a real hindrance sometimes, subjecting you to pleasing people and keeping your image, while seeing little effect upon their lives.

Paul had, by preaching the truth in sacrifice, lost many believers to other teachers who tickled their ears with pleasantries and a less demanding gospel; of which, Paul had to write and fight against constantly. He was never very popular, except to those who loved

God more than life! To them he was nothing less than a precious saint.

There I go preaching again, Bella. Hope you don't mind me rambling on sometimes. Guess this is in place of our lovely walks we used to take, and just share whatever was on our hearts. Bless you all and may God give you joy unspeakable and full of glory! Pray earnestly for me, for I know the battle will be won in the Spirit, not in the flesh.

Saturday, Noon – October 3rd

This week has been a little different but still not all that satisfying. Haven't heard from the owner of the shop on Mill Street as yet, but the large storefront window was smashed by vandals this week. Must keep on trusting the Lord if He wants to give it to me.

The 468 Club was the most inspiring, as I've started a Bible study for each Tuesday morning there. The response was very promising. I could see my efforts of the past eight months of winning their trust and confidence paying off. Twice this week the club would have been closed due to the youth leader being ill, but I volunteered to open it for the lads. The atmosphere on both days was beautiful and peaceful, with much talk of spiritual things. I made pots of tea and bought some biscuits, and I could see the Lord's goodness was having an effect on them. The absence of dirty talk and swearing was notable.

Also, started a Bible study for each Thursday evening at Lydia's house. It was just her and I, but already she is getting excited about people she wants to start inviting. Praise the Lord!

Lydia is a special lady. While working as a cleaning lady at the Florie, she heard about 'The Preacher Man' and wanted to meet me. She was so hungry for the Lord, she accepted Jesus into her heart the first time I spoke with her.

My sister and I have had a heavy burden for Vern, who is dying of cancer. We have set a time to get together with another couple at

Lydia's house tonight, to seek a real touch from God for this man's life. He is the kind of man everybody knows and likes. His healing testimony would not go unnoticed, by any means. On my last visit, I told Vern what we were doing and asked if he was to be healed, would he be sure to give the glory to God. He said yes, he would! His wife was very encouraged to find people who felt their burdens so deeply.

Once again, Bella, I find myself so weak and inadequate in such a situation as this. I ask God to please work in spite of me, for this man's life depends on it.

Had lunch with Mark and his wife last Wednesday, and I enjoyed it very much. He asked if I would identify my ministry to youth as part of St. Gabriel's. I said yes, because it was time to stop feeling the church would bind me. We agreed we all need each other in such a desperate place as this. He and I will get together at 9 a.m. each Monday just to discuss, pray and seek God's guidance for my ministry. Thank you, Lord!

Remember Sarah? The lady who wanted an abortion, then changed her mind? She had a beautiful baby girl. I get to see my miracle baby this afternoon. I'll let you know how things are.

Just laying here enjoying the sounds of a sunny Sunday afternoon filtering through my window. Distant sounds of radios; the barking of dogs; children playing and shouting; all uniquely Liverpool. On a day like this, memories come flooding back. Even the smells bring with them pictures and feelings long forgotten. There is a certain charm about this place when one is given the chance to reflect upon it.

Would you like to go for a walk with me? Well, we shall in spirit, so there!

The service this morning was very good. Mark did a great job of getting a good message across to the unbelievers who came to witness the baptism of two infants. Yes, I felt the Lord there this morning, and if it pleased Him, then it pleases me, too. I brought Lydia and her children, so that was an added blessing. The prayer meeting at her house was very good.

Got to see my little miracle girl yesterday and hold her. Thought to myself, *"If only prospective abortion mothers could hold and look at this, it would end in a day."* So warm and alive and helplessly fragile. Yes, it's much easier when we can't see it. But God has given a woman such a special heart, she could not help but feel the pain, if only she could see it in all its beauty...

My uncle had another stroke, four so far. Such a tragic waste of human life. A perfect example of reaping what you sow (alcohol). Went to see him, but the door for sharing was closed. All I can do is show I care and hope for a break somewhere.

Exhortation

> ***"People! Heaven is at your very fingertips. What is making you so blind? Can't you see the change in me? Don't you want something to happen? Anything, just to make a change? Would you sooner die than call out for help? Is it so hard for you to say you're at the end and in need? Is there yet a small childlike voice inside of you crying out, but can't be heard? Well, I'm listening and I care, but you must cry a little louder so I'll know it's you!"***

It is now evening and I enjoyed my two hour walk. Thought about you most of the time. Got back in time for evening service, but after twenty minutes I got up and walked out. Bella, it was the most boring, dull, lifeless service I have ever been in. When I stepped outside I felt such relief. Sorry if I sound fickle but why should anyone feel obligated to sit there just because they are Christians and be totally bored? If I was feeling down or something, I could blame it on my attitude, but I was just fine. OK, if that's what they are happy with, then I respect that. But I can't take it. Only about a dozen people were there and I think that says it all.

Jesus is Life, Life, Life! So why do they want to settle for less?

Because they are Church of England and that's how they do it! Yet, I keep going back because the people are so neat and friendly, you would just love them all, Bella.

It's been a good day and I shouldn't spoil it with that kind of talk, so there. I'm looking forward to a letter in the morning.

By next weekend I should know if the 468 club will put me on the payroll and, if not, why not. The Florie asked me as a volunteer, to take on manager of one of the football teams and I said no. A long-term commitment may interfere with my desire for full-time employment. So, they are all getting the picture.

Otherwise, it's full-time ministry and I'll live as God provides. But no more full-time voluntary social work. Amen, Bella Rossiter? How come you're so beautiful? Just think, if the Lord doesn't take us home, we have thirty good years ahead of us! Looked at the pictures, and Debbie's blessed me. They say it is better to have loved and lost, than never to have loved at all. But I say it is even better to have loved and won!

Thursday Afternoon, October 8th

My dear Bella,

Thank you for such a great letter. I was definitely having letter withdrawals and don't think I could have lasted much longer. Isn't it funny about our phone calls? When I hang up I still have this big lump in my throat, like I should have gotten rid of it over the phone. My thoughts go something like this. I'm crazy about her and I want to squeeze her tight, and I end up talking about the weather!

It's much like preparing for a sermon. The whole scene flashes before you in living color, exciting, challenging, filled with power and Godly wisdom. Then the moment arrives and your hands are clammy and your tongue is stuck to the roof of your mouth, and you can't even remember the scripture you're supposed to preach on. As your arms hang limp at your side and your voice squeaks out of parched lips, you wonder where that big bold man went that you envisioned the night before.

Well, that isn't exactly how our phone calls are, but I was laughing so hard as I was writing that, because it is so true about my preaching!

Hope this letter doesn't turn out silly, because I'm in a silly mood. If the three of us were together right now, we'd be laughing our silly heads off.

Well, Bella. If you have to be a plump wife, be a happy one. I'm not exactly the curly-headed movie star I used to be, either! Sorry my letters take so long to get to you.

Have a Bible study tonight, and just as I expected, Lydia has four new faces turning up. You can sure tell the difference when a person has been 'born again!' They want others to come and get some. Praise the Lord. And the Bible study at the 468 club was just great. It created a lot of discussion after it was over.

It's 2 p.m. here now and you are just starting your day. You can't wait to get the coffee perking so the aroma can fill the house. You'll sit there sipping and think for a moment about me, and wonder what I'm up to. It's funny, every time I get down or have a bad day, I get more determined to stick it out at any cost. If Satan wants me out, he's going about it all wrong. He should make it nice and pleasant for me here.

God's love is so deep it gets in your veins and runs to every part of the body with your blood. It's impossible to stop it, unless you stop the very life flow of blood.

Now I know I have to quit writing when I come up with things like that, Bella! Just know that all is well, and God has everything under control. Yes, they can even kill my lovely friend, President Sadat, but God is in it. His hand is no less sure, as we enter into the darkest time in history.
We shall look for the appearing of our great God and Savior, Jesus Christ, who alone has the keys to life! In that day, won't our hearts be glad and rejoice that He is ours and we belong to Him. At the

moment of His appearing, every part of our being will be filled with a fire of the Holy Spirit, for the Holy Spirit's job will be finished, and we will see Jesus as He is!

My dearest Bella,

Thank you for that very enjoyable letter which only took four days to get here! I am sitting in my usual Saturday morning restaurant, looking out at the sunny downtown. You could never have guessed last night was torrential downpour and gale force winds that threatened to blow down buildings. Susan's poor little ones were so afraid, they couldn't sleep till mommy came to bed with them.

Vern is slipping away, but I won't give up. Saw him yesterday and encouraged him to stick in there, as we are praying for a miracle. Told his family to believe and not give up, but I can tell they think it's too late. I would give anything to see such a wonderful healing. It would be like the first rays of sunshine after a long cold winter. If God would only show me what to do, I'm sure I would do it. I have never felt so desirous of a thing to happen as I have with this, and all I can do is stand by and watch, and hope, and pray.

Is there a secret, Lord? Tell me before it's too late. Do I believe enough? Then help my unbelief! I truly believe I am nothing and it's all in Your hands!

The Bible study at Lydia's was great. Only one new face, her niece. 'JAWS' was playing on the telly at the same time, so maybe next week we'll have those other faces.

Rex asked me to help with a buffet today as a fund raiser for Vern, so I must get a move on. He and Vern raced pigeons together for many years, thus the interest from Rex.

Allen, the youth leader at 468 club, has assured me a full-time position by December, if I'm still interested by then.

Mark and I have a Monday morning prayer meeting together each week. I told him how awful the Sunday evening service was. So cold and boring, I was unable to sit through it. (Mark was speaking at another church at that time). He said, for me to earn the right to speak out and have people listen to what I have to say, I must never walk out on anything. Otherwise, I give up the right. They will welcome change, but it must come from a mature person, not one who walks out when things don't go his way.

Well, Bella, as you can see, I was humbled and rightly so. I have learned my first big lesson. Praise the Lord.

Letter to My Daughter - November 6, 1981

Hi, my sweet wonderful Debbie,

I'm sitting in my favorite little restaurant with my cuppa, looking out at the deserted streets of downtown Liverpool. Things don't start popping till about nine or ten around here. Then watch out! People get the Christmas fever much earlier than the U.S. And spend like there is no tomorrow. If only it made them happy, I could understand, but it doesn't. Being poor is not acceptable, and pride runs very deep at this time of year.

Well now, your letter sounds like you're doing okay, Deb. Happy with the way Manna is going, (a Christian music group), prospects of a good paying job and three good looking hunks chasing after you! You seem to handle it all very well, and it makes me feel proud of you. Just think! You'll be twenty pretty soon!

In a way, it's exciting to watch your life change and blossom, but in a way it makes me sad. You understand, don't you, Deb. It seems kind of silly...here I am six thousand miles away feeling sad because you'll be leaving home, making a life of your own, and I won't see you much anymore.

But, how I thank God you have become who you are! Once in a while I think how things could have gone the other way, only for Jesus. At those times, my gratefulness to Him moves me deeply, for my love for you has been very deep, indeed.

All my love could never have kept you from the hurts the world had in store for you, but He could and did! Now my lovely girl serves Him and belongs to Him. We are blessed beyond compare. Your children will be blessed, and your children's children. I'd better quit while I'm ahead. I do run at the mouth, don't I, Deb!

Just wrote your mom a few days ago, so I don't want to repeat myself. Had the interview with the 'biggies' of all the youth clubs. I was warned beforehand they don't like anything with religious overtones or moral codes that may rob the youth of his individual feelings! Debbie, if I could have written a script and reenacted it in there, it could not have come out better! My words and explanations moved the whole room, and I realized as I got up to leave, that God Himself had been my portion and my guide.

The room was electrifying, as all faces watched me go. Faces that had never heard or felt quite like that before. Jesus, rather than be left out, had become the only answer to all the needs! Allen, the leader of our 468 club, said they were very impressed. Yet, I had said everything they didn't want to hear! Debbie, never sell God short.

God said *Jesus, His Son*, is the answer for the whole world for all time! We should never slip Him in, but boldly proclaim Him as the answer to every situation. Yet, after saying all that, I must add, use wisdom when dealing with the things of God. We still must be humble, loving, considerate, kind and gentle. For these are the fruit of the Spirit. The true listener will not be turned off, but will be touched by that same Spirit.

I had five people at the Thursday Bible study and it was so good. One was a fourteen year old girl who was constantly running away from home; glue sniffing, etc. I couldn't help thinking, I wish there was someone like you that could take her as a friend. So few dedicated young Christians here and such a harvest! When I think of how many loving girls in your church and music group, I kind of get a little choked up.

I've thought about your singing group and the youth being blessed, yet one more time. I look around here and say, *"If only."* But God in

His wisdom will work all things for His glory, if we faint not. A different country; a different way.

I often dream about the Mill Street property and all the rooms filled with young people like yourself, coming to serve and bring refreshing and hope. Where young can meet young, and be inspired by the love they see day and night. And there will be singing, as a thousand voice choir of angels to our God, and our Lamb, who has given Himself that He may redeem all mankind, and love the lonely and the broken-hearted. Saving moms and dads and bringing peace in the homes that have never known peace or love. Can I be called a fool for dreaming, Deb?

Without a dream or vision there is no hope, so I must go on as a little child awaiting the promise of that happy time to come. *And it will surely come.*

Bless you. I never know how my letters will turn out. But one thing is sure. My love for you. Don't settle for anything less than the real thing, Deb. Just remember, love is a constantly growing thing. So when you start with the real thing, the outcome is more love, peace and joy. I love your mom more each day, till I think I'm going to burst!

Give a big hug in Jesus for me and tell the world you're ready for the fight! All my love to you, Dad

Saturday and Sunday, October 25 & 26 (Psalm 63)

My lovely Bella,

You are my delight and I enjoy knowing you just as a person. Your letters are full of hope and encouraging words from a heart that is full of the childlike love of Jesus. How I thank my God for you, as you fill my needs from so far away. Just know that my love for you runs deep into my very soul. Because my soul is at peace, I have freedom to share it with the poor in spirit who are locked into a never-ending prison. That is, till they cry out and the Lord of glory sets them free.

Isn't it great, Bella, to be free! To be in the world, free to love and share and comfort the oppressed; yet not of the world! Shielded and protected by the lover of our souls. Praise God for giving us new life! People can't understand why we have no pleasure in those things that they enjoy, for our eyes have been opened by the God of truth, while they are still fooled by the father of lies.

Last Thursday I had my Bible study at Lydia's. I came away so full because of what the Lord is doing in Lydia's life. Rex saw my joy and the Bible under my arm and started to provoke me. But I had been filled and he could not touch that which was flowing inside of me. Hate confronted love and wanted to put out that light. Because the light penetrated the dark to reveal the hidden things deep within. I felt like Stephen in the Bible as I walked away, leaving a raging bull who had lost all control, full of hate. I only felt sorrow for him, Bella, because his family watched the whole thing. I'm sure they felt only shame for their father.

The 468 club is going well. Sometimes I get impatient with the Lord, till He shows me He is doing a deep work in these boys. The problems they have are so rooted in bitterness from the day they are born. Only the tenderest love and care will produce lasting fruit. One young man, Bobby, was disliked by all for his violent outbursts of temper and total disdain for others and their feelings. But, rather than being turned off, I seemed to be drawn to him. At first, he would have nothing to do with me, but that didn't seem to matter to me. I can't honestly say why I liked him, but I found I was doing little things just for him. Over a period of time, we had formed an unspoken bond that now, I'm quite sure, he would go out of his way to please me. His respect for me is obvious to all.

Yesterday morning, Danny and I were alone in the club when Bobby came in. So we made a nice cup of tea and pooled all our pennies together and got some cakes. It was a special time that comes along only once in a while. It was perfect. As Bobby found himself sharing his memories of a life so cruel to him, it made me want to cry. It was the most touching story I have ever heard, and I felt such compassion for him. Bella, his dad found out Bobby wasn't his child, and at six weeks old he battered him in his crib. He was put in a home for four years just to keep him away from his dad's hate and wickedness towards him. As a small boy, he couldn't make a sound when dad was in the house, so he just cowered in a corner, hoping he hadn't done anything wrong.

One time he was picked up over his dad's head and thrown through a closed window. As he lay crumpled up in the back garden, his dad picked him up by the throat, dangling him in mid-air and told him one day he's going to dig a hole right there and bury him alive! Now I know why I was drawn to him; it was Jesus reaching out through me, without me ever knowing why.

This last three weeks have been particularly hard for me - *"ye of little faith"* - feeling sorry for myself. As I have already mentioned, I gave the money from the sale of the mini-bus away. I've been broke for the last three weeks. Yes, it was easy to forget the wonderful feeling I got when meeting those needs. I took my eyes off the Lord, as I wondered why nobody would think that I, too, have needs. Such simple lessons I need to learn over and over again! Proverbs 3:5-6.

The shop is still there. That's in God's hands. Vern is about the same. Last time I went to see him, I held his hand and prayed. Couldn't help thinking it would have been impossible to get that close to him if he wasn't sick. Oh God, that you would grant me this man's life as a gift for me to enjoy forever! Sarah and baby are doing just fine. The Keith Green booklet was excellent, Bella. He is such a beautiful Christian and witness for the Lord. Such a clear and uncomplicated view of the true Christian walk.

I have some soft worship music on and the house is empty. I love the quiet of a Sunday afternoon. Church was nice and friendly, but I don't ever feel the Lord there, so I don't much look forward to the evening service; so I end up not going. Mark, bless his friendly heart, doesn't understand why I feel this way.

I should have called you because it's been two weeks since I last wrote. Maybe I'll surprise you during the week! This is my last sheet of paper, so I can't get too mouthy. Boy, the joy in my heart to think I'll see you all soon. I'll never make a good missionary. I'm too soft.

But the future belongs to us. Happy are they whose joy is the Lord.

November 4th, 9 a.m.

My dearest Bella,

Thank you for the money and encouraging letters. I hope I don't sound repetitive when I say you are truly a blessing to me beyond words. I wish all men could find the joy, peace and contentment in a relationship as I have found in you. As I trace my life in meeting you, I find myself saying, could it have been all by accident? By chance? No! Something this beautiful could only have come from God, the giver of all good things. Even before I knew Him? Yes! For His love is not bound to time; His mercies are from eternity; His wisdom is past finding out. Surely God made you and me for this very moment in time! What can separate you and me from the love of God, when He formed us with His very own hands? That same Lord chose to take Vern last Thursday, and who am I to argue. Praise His Holy Name...

All is going well here, Bella. Lydia is a joy to watch as she grows in her love and understanding of Jesus. She is as hungry as a lion for the things of God and is constantly on the lookout for people to share what she has found. She is reading books to encourage her in the baptism and will not be put off. She wants me to start a Bible study for children. I think I'll wait till after the Christmas holiday, so I can give it my full attention.

My Monday prayer time with Mark was super! We had such joy in the Lord. He told me Nicky Cruz has requested to come to Toxteth for a crusade in April. Mark has been contacted to do some of the groundwork. He asked if I would help him. Would I! I would spend myself, I am so happy. This time I'm going to get Nicky by himself and have a good chat if it kills me. Praise God for the joy and excitement of this life!

It will be good to give Susan some money. She has been so faithful to me. I don't mention the children very often, but rest assured, we have a grand time together. I take them to church whenever they show signs of wanting to go.

I don't witness or ask my family to meetings; just love them and let my life be the witness. They have heard it all so much before. Now it's up to them and I have total peace in it. Times are hard on these people, and I know God is gentle and patient with them.

I go for another interview for the 468 club job tomorrow, but it's a formality, as they want me for sure. But, it has to be open for all. I feel so good in my spirit for these clubs. God has given me such love. The way they all have taken to me is only from God's hand. How can I fail with such a wide open door of acceptance? I know I could never have pulled it off alone.

Had a long talk with Jim R. I called collect but he didn't seem to mind. Whew! Seems he needed more info on the Mill Street property before confronting others about it, so I was able to fill him in. He recommends putting the property in a non-profit trust instead of my name, in case there is a time I may sell it. Those that financed it will have a say in where the money should be used. That would prevent me from benefiting from it for my own personal use.

Does it sound like Jim? I said I would, but the more I think about it the more I feel like telling him not to bother. We have become so business oriented, we miss the simplest act of sharing in the Lord's work; turning it into the world's system of covering all the angles. Faith in God's children never seems to be enough. But, I'll leave that for now and pray on it before saying much more.

Wednesday, November 11th

My dearest Bella,

I've eagerly looked forward to a letter from you since Saturday. Well, maybe tomorrow, girl. I guess I'm in need of that constant touch from home. I love you all so much and feel that empty place so strongly at certain times.

It's blustery winds and rain today, typical English weather. Monday prayer with Mark was excellent again. He asked me to visit a Vietnam boat family, which I was very happy to do. It was just the young wife at home, and it took her some time to trust me to open the door and allow me in. They had been so mistreated here, I could hardly blame her. But my winning smile and honest face won the day, cough, cough! Poor girl, couldn't understand a word of English or speak but a few words. I was soon lying on the floor with pen and paper drawing all my little messages. It was quite funny really, and I sensed her relaxing and enjoying it. She was Buddhist and never had heard of Jesus. It was quite a challenge to introduce to her in sign language, a message completely alien to her. I think the Lord did a fine job. She thinks her family would like to visit my church this Sunday. I'll visit again tonight when her husband is home.

I've been reading the *Apocryphal Books* of the New Testament that Mark gave me. What a bunch of garbage the first three turned out to be! Mary, the blessed most holy virgin, born of the Holy Spirit just as Jesus was? The childhood of Jesus and some of the mean things He did! Rubbish, all of it. How can they do this to Him? One book was quite interesting, as it gave a more detailed account of Jesus' trial, death and resurrection, without casting any shadow on the Authorized Version. Then some letters from Paul, which are quite good, but they miss the spiritual depth we have come to know and love from Paul.

Even a mere babe in Christ as I am, I am able to see the lack of holy inspiration in these books. I'm far from finished, as the complete volume is larger than the whole New Testament. Already, I am happy with the Word as we know it. I would not dream of adding a word of this other to it! But in order to sit with others of a different persuasion, I need to know the facts. Don't know why I even told you all that, Bella. Forgive me if I get boring at times.

Thursday Bible study is growing, thanks to Lydia. That girl is in love with Jesus and it's full speed ahead. She figures there should be eleven, possibly more, if they all show up. I feel I need to continue to teach them to be a light unto this world, which is in such darkness. Their lives must shine brighter than the lights of yesterday. To end up with such a sad world, our lives as Christians must have been awful dim. If we don't expect God to do great things, He won't.

"Turn your eyes upon Jesus. Look full in His wonderful face. And the things of earth will grow strangely dim, in the light of His glory and grace."

Saturday Morning, November 21st

My dearest lovely Bella,

It is always so good when I hear your voice on the phone. It was so cute how we started laughing. All our pent-up feelings seemed to release in those few moments, didn't they? It's going to be a wonderful Christmas, enjoying my special family again. I have learned to enjoy the simple things in life that most people take for granted, and very often abuse. I've come to appreciate to the depth of meaning in the word love since leaving you and our family behind.

Can't say enough about the Thursday night Bible study. One woman was so blessed we now have one in her home with new faces. I'll fill you in on all the details when I see you. My permanent position is secure at the 468 club for when I get back. Praise our God for His wisdom. Then the Florie offered me a job for thirty pounds more, but I turned it down. I feel at peace with my choice.

Haven't heard back from Jim R. yet, concerning the Mill Street property, but I'm sure I will not accept a gift on his terms. I'm sure we will have time to talk when I am home.

Well, Bella, my love. Seeing as I will be with you soon, I find myself not wanting to go into much detail about things here. I guess that's normal, isn't it? My heart and mind are already with you. It's just a matter of days I have to plod through till I leave. It's a little bit like school the last couple of weeks before summer vacation. Nobody feels like getting too involved so close to the end.

PART II

1982

Back in Liverpool
4 a.m. Sunday Morning, January 3, 1982

Hello my lovely,

My last glimpse of you and Deb at the airport made me realize fully what it was costing you to let me go again. You looked so vulnerable, it was all I could think about the whole time of the trip. You are not a super woman, as some may think; you are just a woman who said, *yes, I'll bear the pain, if this is the way it has to be.*

I can hear Jesus more clearly now: *"Father! If there be any other way..."* He knew there wasn't before He asked, the pain made Him ask just one more time. I want you to know, Bella, I know how much it's costing you, but it's still worth the price. I love you and thank you for all the special ways you are to me. I tell you from the mouth of my Father, your reward is great in the Kingdom of Heaven, for you have given much. If I wanted someone to reach the ears and heart of God for me, it would no doubt be you; so pray for me and it shall be done!

My flight was very smooth but I got no sleep. The movie was good, but the soft music on the earphones was better. I was able to relax and think about our Christmas time together. The plane touched down about noon, and I got to the station about 2 p.m. Had to wait till 5:30 for a train out, so I took in some of the sights. I must have looked pretty bad, because the girl sitting next to me on the train to Liverpool thought I was suffering the effects of New Year's Eve! Did she ever get a surprise when I shared where I had been and where I was going, all because of what Jesus had done for me.

Got home at nine and scared Susan half to death. The kids missed me so much I got all kinds of hugs and kisses. They had to show me all their toys from Christmas. I was so tired, but they were having so much fun, I couldn't complain. Finally, I took a bath, but the water went cold and had to jump out before I was finished. My room was freezing and the little heater had broken down. I put all my clothes back on and dove into bed. Slept till one p.m. the next day.

After giving Susan some money for my keep, I am broke again. But don't worry none. It is easy to be without here. I just blend in very nicely. Visited with Lydia and kids. So many people are coming to her in need, she plumb wore herself out. Started to carry their burdens too deeply, and didn't have time to pray or read her Bible. I was able to put things in perspective and take the load off her shoulders before she went down.

It's Sunday and I'm not sure I want to go to church, but I'd better wait and see what the Lord says about that. It's important that Mark find me a willing friend, even if I don't like his church.

I'm enjoying *'Cry of the Human Heart.'* There are so many things in it I need to apply to my life that is so vital to the work here.

They had a tremendous snowfall after I left for the U.S., bringing much of the air traffic to a halt. If I'd have waited to leave any later than I did, it may have been very difficult, especially on standby. Thank you, Lord!

Good morning again, Bella,
Was up at six. I want to get some semblance of a routine as soon as possible. It's easy to get depressed after a nice time with you guys, and then see all the bleakness and problems here. My spirit is willing, but my flesh is weak!

I did go to church and it was okay. Felt close to the Lord at communion time. *"Rejoice in the Lord always and again I say, rejoice!"*

Monday Morning – January 11th

Dear Bella,

It is freezing! The coldest and worst winter in thirty years! The snow is frozen solid on the ground. Many parts of the country are under flood water. I decided to stay in my warm bed this morning and write to my lovely girl. I sure do miss you. Hope you are doing okay, Bella. It's been ten days since I left you. I'm dying to get my first letter from you.

I've had a full week between the 468 club, the Florie, Bible study and visiting. Went to see Mr. Linsford about the Mill Street property and got the cold shoulder. Was told to come back in a half hour. I walked through the park wishing this guy was a little more friendly. I prayed the Lord would soften him up, or I couldn't face him again. When I got back, he was a changed person, so we had a lovely chat! He didn't turn down my offer of fifty quid a week, but left it up to the real estate agent to work out a deal. They're not crazy about my offer, but want to see me today to come to some kind of arrangement.

The Bible study went well. One woman is going through divorce. Her husband found another woman and is spending all the money on booze. A very common story here. She has come to the study in search of help, and I want the Lord to help her.

Remember I told you the story about Bobby? He was the one who had the terrible life with his dad. After the riots, a magazine did an article on the youth of this area, and he was chosen for an interview. Some family in Europe read the article and sent him a check for eighty pounds and he was really touched. Wants me to write a thank you letter for him. His electricity had been cut off before Christmas for non-payment, so he went without heat, lights or T.V. over the holidays. Now he wants to use that money to pay the bill. He is beginning to see there's good in the world and it's changing him.

Want to do the 'American' thing at the club till I'm permanent next month. Told Allen I'm going to scrub and redecorate the whole club so the boys can feel good about their place. I think they will have a tendency to respect it if it's done in good taste. I'm trying out new ideas like trusting them with things they couldn't be trusted with before. I've been warned many times that they will take advantage of me, but they have never failed me yet. Took four of them for a drive the other night just for something to do, and guess where we ended up? At Aunt Millie's house in Woolton. Don't know what possessed me to take them there, but she just loved them to death with cups of tea and 'chocky bickies.'

Took a couple of the boys to Lydia's house and she fussed over them, too. So they are getting to see me and my friends and hearing how we live with the Lord.

The sun is streaming right through my window and I can't wait to get out. It's going to be a great day. Praise the Lord for all His kindness to you and me. *We love Him because He first loved us!*

January 16th

My lovely Bella,

Thank you for your lovely letter. It's great to get one on Saturday morning, because that's my favorite day for writing to you. I sent you one a couple of days after I arrived back and again a week later, so you should be getting both soon. I love you very much and I too, feel that lost and lonely feeling sometimes. No matter how busy I get, there is still a void that only you can fill. One day at a time is all I can see. That way I don't think of us as separated for a long time.

You are not alone in your spiritual feelings being elusive, Bella. We have passed from the excitement of learning about Jesus to living for Him. What a reality! The disciples must have enjoyed the spark of newness and wonder, as they walked and learned with Jesus each day. Such crowds! Such miracles! Such wonders to behold, as sickness and death vanished by a touch or a word from His lips! Who wouldn't follow such a one as this, especially with the promise of them doing the same! But, Jesus went ahead and spoiled it all by letting them nail Him to a tree! He could have been the King and we along with Him, healing all the world from a place of authority. Bringing peace and harmony forever to a sick and hurting world. But no, He had to do it the hard way, and we all have to suffer and die for the faith. *Thank you, God, for your wisdom.* There is not a man who ever lived who would have done it Your way, and we would never have known to what depth you would have gone to win us back. You set the highest price, and paid it in full when You could have chosen an easier way. We would have regretted that day. For a little while we suffer, but, oh, the joy when we come face to face! We see now as in a hazy mirror, but then we will understand and rejoice at the magnificent plan that was laid out before time began.

Sorry I got carried away again, Bella. When I start writing I never know what's going to come out.

The weather has been awful. I am now up to wearing three pairs of socks; honest! My poor shoes are bulging at the seams and my feet are still freezing! Everywhere is a mass of solid ice and snow. It looks like the Russian North. It is comical to see what I jump into bed in. You would think I was going out for a hike!

I had five of the boys in my room the other night, all huddled around my one bar electric heater. Nobody wanted to move or go home, so we stayed for about four hours telling stories. It took me a week to defrost 'Debbie 2' (a little mini car I had bought). It was frozen solid. So, last night the boys put some gas in it for me and I took them for a drive. We had only gone a mile when the radiator sprung a leak, and we lost all our precious anti-freeze. All the stations we went to had frozen pipes, so we ended up stuffing snow in the radiator and made it back home!

In one way, the weather has been a blessing. Rather than stand on the street corner freezing, some of the boys have come up to Lydia's and helped me paint her house. Most of the time they ended up playing games with her children and drinking gallons of tea. But I do manage to get a little work out of them.

I did get to see the real estate agent who informed me it would be easier if I had two hundred pounds down, but would see what he could do, anyway. So, once again, it's in the Lord's hands.

Sunday Morning, 24th

My dear Bella,

I got two letters from you this week and I loved them. I am living in an unreal world and you bring me back to reality. Such a hard, difficult life here; full of unsolved problems. Yet, for some strange reason, I want to stay on for the battle; to fight till I can't fight any more. The enemy is so entrenched here, much of my time is taken up fighting him.

Rex's son, Billy, has suddenly become attached to me of late, along with a handful of young 'scallies'. We have been fixing up 'Debbie 2' and going for rides or helping to paint Lydia's house. Now, I hear Rex is angry with his son for not spending time and helping him! His son doesn't like his dad and has been staying at his brother's house out of fear. Rex's daughter is again showing an interest in going to America, so I'm walking on egg shells.

Brenda has come to the Bible study twice and is starting to respond. Her husband, who drinks all the dole money up and is openly seeing another woman, does not like the change in his wife. She is standing up and demanding some changes. His response is, *"One of these days I'm coming up to this 'religious sex orgie' and sort things out!"*

One man who works with Lydia at the Florie attributed the change in Lydia's life to '*more than Bible studies',* and in a careless moment, made some damaging statements. By the time I got wind of it, the damage was done. Many thoughtless youth, whom I have given so much of my time to, now found it a game to throw in little innuendos to see what my response would be. They were only acting out of an empty heart and an empty life. But, the man that started it, I decided he should not get off free and should know the damage he had done.

With the Florie manager, Reg Ash, as a referee, I confronted the man with it. I made him see the evil he had caused. It was a humbling experience for a man who wasn't used to being humbled, but all the sorrow in the world couldn't undo what had been done.

When the light shines in a dark place, men will try to put out that light, for it reveals the evil in their hearts. With all humility of heart, Bella, and by the grace of God, I say they have never been exposed to a life such as mine. If Satan succeeds in putting out this light, he will have made a big mistake. In Jesus, I have touched too many hearts and it will never be put out, but will shine even brighter.

The Mill Street property looks like a dead issue. He wants cash and there are interested buyers, so I will just leave it there. I have done all I can, so the Lord must have something better. I find myself indulging in self-pity once in a while, but it doesn't last long. Every inch to be won is a battle that is sometimes swept away in minutes.

Monday Morning, 25th

I did plan on finishing this yesterday, but Danny wanted driving lessons and needed me to write out two end-of-the-year reports for him. I'll be taking his job at the club next week.

After reading over what I had written Sunday, I got to thinking you may feel all is a big struggle; but, I have to say, no. There are many happy moments. Most of all, I feel I am doing what my whole life has been leading up to doing. I was the one that got away to discover and live a new life in a new country. But, on top of that, I discovered the real meaning to life in Jesus.

If God has given me a gift, it must be, *"I am all things to all men, that I may win some."* I have never forgotten what it feels like to be like them. If I do get a meeting place started, it will be like no other church, for it will reflect the personality of the local people. Jesus will meet them just where they are.

I read your letters through many times, Bella, so all your news is lovingly appreciated. If only you could see yourself as I see you, you wouldn't feel frustration at all. Just enjoy being you. You are fantastic beyond compare – ask your own children! For you to feel less than contentment is pure robbery. In all my life I have never met one who I admire more than you!

Sunday, January 30th, 1982

Well, my love,

No letter from you this week! Sure do miss it, but I guess I'll survive. Had an interesting week, to say the least. Went on a three-day camp-out with the 468 club, and it was great. A tough Army sergeant set the whole thing up with all the equipment, and went along to show us how to use it, and to teach us map and compass reading. Also, how to scale cliffs Army-style with a rope. After setting up the gear for absailing (cliff scaling), nobody would go over but him, because it scared the hell out of us all!

On our way to the village the next day, we passed over a hundred-foot bridge. For a joke, one of the boys said he would have a go at absailing over it. Scotty, the Sarge, stopped the bus and started setting up the rope, as the lad stood by shaking in his boots. Bell, I could hardly look over, let alone climb over and scale down. You know what I'm like! But, to cut a long story short, Scotty was so good with us, we all ended up having a go! It was the thrill of my life! I did something I never thought I could do. Thinking back on it gives me the willies, but I'm sure I'd do it again.

The first time I met Scotty, I didn't care for him because of his way of speaking to the boys, swearing and stuff. But during the camp-out, we became real good friends. I was able to share my testimony of what the Lord had done for me. He was genuinely interested, asking many questions.

One time around the campfire, we got around to talking about Heaven. I said if I got there first, I would be praying for the rest of them to make it. One of the boys said, *"Don't pray for me. All my friends are in the other place."* That got the usual big laugh. Then out of the blue, Scotty said, *"Pray for me, Frank. I'd like to go there."* It was a great moment, as all eyes turned to the tough Sergeant. I said, *"I will, Scotty."*

One night we all piled into the village pub. I brought the guitar along and we had a great sing-along with the usual Johnny Cash songs and Beatles favorites. Then I started singing *'Amazing Grace'* amidst a few protesting voices. Then Scotty joined in, then Danny, then Fred. Then the barmaid joined in the singing. What a feeling!

I had promised to hitch-hike home with Fred (he was newly wedded, so still in love) but everybody put up such a protest, Fred had to leave without me. What a dilemma. They want me with them all the time, yet they make out they don't want what I've got?

I start work Monday. Praise the Lord! It's been a long year of struggle, most of the time without money. I think I'll enjoy getting a regular pay check for a change. This next year, I feel will be interesting, using my imagination and starting new projects. The first thing I want to do is clean up the club, and try to encourage the boys to take a little pride in it for their own comfort. I'll try to fill you in on each day's progress. Maybe I'll have a quiet hour each morning to do some writing, as most of the youth don't come too much before noon.

Talking about writing, Bella. Guess what! Billy took my manuscript to read and was sharing some bits with his dad. He asked his dad if he wanted to read it next and dad said no. I saw Billy yesterday, and he was overjoyed. He said, *"Guess what, Frank. My dad is reading it!"* Small miracles, I love them. I still sometimes wish I was a Dave Wilkerson and could see these kids come to Jesus in a dynamic way, but it looks like a long hard road ahead.

Be patient with me, Bella, and we'll see the end. I feel like crying sometimes, because I am just me. But this is all I have. God knows He must do the miracles. I make a great youth leader, but that alone would never make me happy. Pray for a real anointing for me. To be a light is not enough for me here. It will take the moving of the Holy Spirit to convict and set these people free to stand for Jesus.

Fred is a good example. He loves me and wants it all, but he's bound up by his image. Nineteen year old Lorraine is the same way. Danny is another. Rex's boy is so tender, but! *"Who will I identify with?"* they want to know. I could go on and on about the people who want to, but! So I wait patiently and wonder when the dam will break, and why I can't bring them on home.

Two weeks ago, a Christian lady promised to visit with Lydia and make friends. She has yet to do it. So I get the reputation of having an affair, because I'm the only one available to be a friend and encourage her. But the Lord knows we are free from this kind of relationship, and Satan can have his day. But, this work will go on, because it's having its effect on Satan's territory. I thank God for every word of slander and accusation, for I must be close to victory. *"He opened not His mouth..."* And neither will I. He knew where

He was going and why, and so do I. In the end, He will not be my Judge, but my Friend! He will keep me from the wicked one, just as He did Peter. Paul said, *"When I am weak, then I am made strong in Him."*

Well, my love. Monday seems so far away to wait for a letter. I wonder if I should call you today. I need to hear your voice. Bless you all for being my family. A warm glow of contentment for you.

Midnight, Tuesday, February 2nd

My dearest lovely Bella,

The phone call was so painful. Such a helpless feeling overwhelmed me. I sat in a daze for a long time. When I finally did go down to the main room of the club, it was a shambles. The boys had gotten to messing around and one thing led to another. Someone set the fire extinguisher off, and it was still gushing water all over everything when I walked in. I felt such anger and frustration, I screamed at everyone to get out. I called them a bunch of animals, fit only for the gutter. Then I locked the door and sat and stared at the damage. My second day on the job, and I felt I was through. I had worked so hard those two days, cleaning and making the place so nice, and in ten minutes, they had destroyed it. I felt I couldn't face another day.

I got to thinking how much you needed me, and here I sat among the rubble, empty, while you were hurting so much, and how you were much more important than anything here. I had changed the Bible study to tonight because of my work schedule, and wished with all my heart I was a thousand miles from here. I knew I had to face it. Danny came home with me and we had dinner in my room. Then he came to the study with me. Fred came a short time later. I prayed in earnest for the Lord to touch you in a deep way, and give us both back the vision we once had. Otherwise, I would have to leave.

Well, my love, that was the best Bible study yet! Fred and Danny just came alive. They couldn't stop talking and shared all the little changes going on inside since they met me. Things that were personal to them and hard to talk about. They talked about if I went back, it would leave a big hole in their lives. They mentioned all the little changes they had noticed in the other boys at the club, too. Once again, they shared the joy they felt when they saw me coming over the hill on the camp-out, when they thought I wouldn't come back from my U.S. visit. Now they were not ashamed to admit their deepest feelings, and I was deeply touched. They believed everything I said about God, but believing and not receiving made them frustrated. They didn't think they could face the mockery that would surely follow.

So, in my deepest moment of despair, Bella, God had shown me the hidden work that was going on. The work that He alone was aware of, and I knew I could not go back. That night in bed, I realized I would have to lay you on the altar, too. The last barrier had been broken. *"Any man who puts his hand to the plow and looks back, is not fit to be my disciple."* God would have to meet your needs and give you the strength to go on without me, and I, you.

Saturday Morning

You called me Wednesday! Is that not an answer to prayer! God is so good and you are so lovely! He knows you are able to take it. He has confidence in you, and so do I. Don't be ashamed of your feelings of weakness, Bella. God was aware of all that before He called you into this life. What's important is He is able to carry you through.

I have had a terrific week at the club. The atmosphere of the whole place has changed; even Allen, the youth leader, is amazed. I cooked breakfast at the club yesterday morning for eight of us, and it was great. We all pitched in and bought bacon, eggs, hash browns and fresh baked rolls from the bakery. I fixed a nice table up without realizing they felt embarrassed at the idea of eating like this. They were not used to eating at a table at home, let alone with all their friends. They did it for me, because they could see I did it all to please them, and didn't want to hurt me. Bunch of softies, I say! After breakfast, they even pitched in to clean up! Billy helped me to cook, and he felt so pleased with himself.

Well, I could go on forever, Bella, of the blessings of the Lord, but I'd better quit for now. We did go absailing again, and it was good seeing Scotty again. He wants to read my manuscript too as soon as I can get it to him. Watch out, Lord, the old tough Sergeant is on his way!

Friday, February 12th

Well, my sweet Bella,

Got my first paycheck yesterday! Fifty-five pounds. Not much, I know, but it's good to have a steady income after a year of the other. Susan can breathe a little easier too, as she got herself into a bit of debt. I give her twenty-five pounds, and I take care of the rental payments on the telly. Bought myself a good egg pan for five pounds, as I'm starting to cook for the boys at the club. My first breakfast went great, till I started cooking the eggs, thus the reason for my very own egg pan.

Made chicken and cheese omelets this morning for Billy and another youth; kind of private like. When the others found out about it, they went mad. Thought I'd start hitting the local butchers for some free bones and make fresh soup every day.

A funny thing happened the other day. I was explaining to the boys what bowling was like, as none had ever done it before. Suddenly, I got a brainstorm and called the one and only bowling alley, which happened to be in New Brighton, across the Mersey River. *"Sir,"* I said, *"I've got a group of unemployed youth who have never even seen a bowling alley, let alone play in one. Would you allow me to come out there and teach them how to do it?"* Well, Bella, he gave all the usual excuses why that wasn't possible. They were just barely keeping their heads above water. So, I let him have it. *"I'm not trying to run your business, but it seems to me, the more you expose the game to people, the more people will want to play it. What they don't know, they won't miss. Who knows, I may be the one to initiate leagues between the youth clubs of Liverpool!"*

He told us to come on over and he'll see what he can do! So eight of us jumped into the mini-bus, and when we got there the whole show was free; shoes and all. The boys loved it and want to do it again. The trouble is, Bella, it's too expensive. 25p to get in, 25p for shoes, and 75p for every game. I made sure we all thanked the manager for his kindness. If we do get something going on a regular basis, he'll have to work out a cheaper deal for these lads. It's better to do that than let the lanes stand idle most of the day, don't you think? They would also make money off the cafe' and game machines.

The Bible study was very good again. Because my job is so demanding, I find I'm pressured to be ready for the study. But, God has always been faithful to give me some very beautiful things to share without long hours of preparation. Lydia's faith is growing so deep and strong, she is quite a witness to all who knew her before. Her children are enjoying the new life, too. God is dealing with everybody who comes. There is no compromise, but it is done in love. Whoever comes to Jesus will be aware of the cost and the joy.

I don't have a Bible study at the club at this time, but His light and witness is there. All our talks and discussions are interjected with Christian ideas. Not a day goes by without the Lord giving me a deepening relationship with someone in the club. My enjoyment comes from the positive response and respect they have toward me. There is none that is closed to me now. Just a total open friendship. I couldn't hurt any one of them or they me. When I find I'm overwhelmed by it all, I often ask the Lord, how can this be? I thought this kind of relationship with the ungodly came only by compromise. So, I search for some, but there is none. It is His gift for me to enjoy. But there will be troubled times ahead.

He is showing me the perfect way to love, but the cost will be realized in the end. And the fruit, mmm, so tasty. If none ever came to Jesus, my feelings for them would not change a bit. I do what I do because I feel it's in me to do. No gimmicks, no reasons, no expectations. The Lord's work is His alone, my job is just to be me. My! What a relief. No pressures to perform, no heads to count. *"Thank you, Lord, for saving my soul! I can't remember anyone twisting my arm, but I do remember You touching my heart. Touch these boys when you're ready and I won't be too far away."*

Well Bella, my sweet wife. I want so much to hear from you. You have been such a part of my life, I can't get used to being without you.

Next Morning

No letter! But I still love you! Beautiful sunny morning. Keep looking up! I'm doing some street ministry today with some new Christians I met.

Saturday, February 21st

Dear Bella,

What a special woman you are. Your letter was so full of love and tenderness, it warmed me up inside. Not even the biting cold outside could rob it from me as I walked to the bus stop. This is my kind of Saturday; when I can enjoy your closeness, writing and receiving from each other. On this day, it's just us, and I think of nothing else but you.

I look forward to our week together and plan to rent a car for that week. I have always wanted to visit Devon and Cornwall, so I will look over a map and make a note of some of the places to go. Let's take three or four days and just enjoy each other and the beautiful country God has given us here. Maybe we could come back to Liverpool by way of the coast of Wales; it has such beauty.

He, in His goodness, has kept me from all evil, so that, having done all, I can stand. Love these people with me, Bella, for your sacrifice is far greater than mine. Enjoy the fruits of your labor and see them as our Lord and Savior sees them. Let your light shine, if only for a couple of days, so they may see the beauty and love I know so well.

I have finished my third week at the club and it is so great. The changes there are nothing short of a miracle. I am now ready to do a personal profile on each of the boys the way I see them. I want each one to read his and discuss it with me over a cup of tea, in private. I am beside myself with happiness at what our lovely God is doing in and through me; and the change in you compounds the joy. Is it right for me to feel such joy? Yes, I love it!

How can I be full of a million things to say and not be able to write them! Because writing is so slow and my mind is racing on. Forgive me if I end this letter, for I know I will see you soon and we can talk our heads off.

Your last letter took six days, the one before took fourteen! I'm sure you will give me all the details of your arrival and such. So, knowing you, I won't even worry.

Took Lydia to that beautiful church in the Dingle. Remember the one we had to climb over the gate because they lock it up once the service starts? The pastor is a real down to earth Liverpool guy that I felt could speak the same language as the street kids. So I went back for a chat. After listening to me, he said, *"Frank, I would love to open this church and minister to the youth, but the church won't have it. They love from a distance, but they worry about the beautiful building and the damage that can be done. That's why they lock the gates."* He told me he came here two years ago filled with the Holy Ghost fire, but now he finds it harder to get excited. He got into a rut because he couldn't move the people, so he said to me, *"Don't look for a church – you are the church in the youth club and in homes for Bible study. That's the only church they need now. The churches will never meet their needs because the churches live in their own little world; they feel safer that way."*

I went away a little sad but with a different picture. The words, *"You are the church"* had a special ring to them and for the first time I saw its meaning. The church is the active force within a community. A force or people not tied to a building, but who carry the love of Christ everywhere. We have become afraid to say church is boring, like it would hurt God to hear the truth. If people in a building don't have the excitement of Christ and the realization of an everyday walk with Him, then it will be boring. If Jesus is exciting within me, then I must be part of that church walking around letting Christ love the world. Touching, talking, caring, doing. He never meant us to stagnate in a building, but only to use that building to express the joy we feel within.

Don't think I did a good job of explaining that, but I know how I feel and that's what counts.

Saturday Morning

Hi, sweetheart,

What a beautiful morning! So crisp, bright and quiet. Had a lovely stroll to town and couldn't help thinking, *"Lord, you look so much better in the sunshine and it's so much easier to smile..."* It's been a storybook spring for us here, Bella. Most of the week has been this way.

Last Sunday, while having a time with the Lord, Scotty, the Sarge, kept coming to mind. I felt the Lord prompting me to share with him in a definite way. On Tuesday, I invited him to have breakfast with me at the youth club. It was great, Bella. I cooked bacon and cheese omelets and for two hours we talked about spiritual things. My feeling was right. He has been giving it a lot of thought since he met me. His wife wants to invite me for dinner, for she too, is interested. I would never have known all this if I hadn't stepped out in faith to the Lord's prompting. I want to praise His Name! By the way, Scotty did make the effort to come down to meet you, but couldn't locate where I lived.

One major reason Fred gave for not giving God his life was the living with in-laws. If only he could have a fresh start someplace else, he would have time to grow without too much pressure. Well, he and his beautiful bride have just been given a great little remodeled house and they are thrilled. Our God has a way of knocking all the props away, doesn't He, Bella.

Danny is doing fine. Having acquired 'Debbie 2" from me, it has given him a closer link with his wife and children. He would rather put petrol in the car than spend the little he has on beer. He has become very thoughtful of late.

At the Bible study, we are studying the fruit and gifts of the precious Holy Spirit, whom I seem to be more aware of lately. Praise God for that! They are getting a firm foundation that will enable them to stand on our Jesus and Him alone. Two Mormons came to visit Lydia, so she ran down to get another lady from the Bible study for support. Talk about a glowing account of God's faithfulness to His new babes. They literally put those guys to shame. The Mormons keep running into more people I am personally involved with. My name is becoming something of a thorn to them.

Toxteth people know and trust me, even though many are not Christians, making it very difficult for the Mormons to operate. Without even trying, I became a standard against them. Praise God for His wisdom!

I have chosen not to go to France with the 468 club. Allen has been gracious to let me drop out. The Nicky Cruz Crusade will be here then, and also I would miss my Bible study which I must be faithful to at all costs. I want to be here to stir up interest in Nicky, maybe buy a few of his books to pass out.

On April 12th I have been invited to minister in song at the Full Gospel Businessmen's dinner in Southport. The Lord has given me such an excitement for this. The dinner is eight dollars (four pounds) for each who attend. A lot of money, but I feel strongly about inviting Scotty and wife, Danny and wife, Fred and wife, and three or four other couples. I will ask Allen for the use of the mini-bus for that evening. It will be my expense, but I will ask Full Gospel to help. Pray for this time, Bella. Please don't forget.

Sunday, March 14th

My dear Bella,

It's four p.m. dark and rainy. Does that sound familiar to you? I haven't left my room all day except to eat dinner, so I'm writing this in bed. Don't seem to want to see anybody for a while, just want to be alone with my thoughts.

After leaving you at the airport, a deep sadness came over me and I cried most of the long ride home. I couldn't get the image out of my mind how helpless and lonely you sounded facing that unfamiliar long trek home. I felt like I'd abandoned you. Real or imagined, I will never do that again. I went to bed as soon as I got home so I didn't have to think of you stranded in St. Louis alone. I ended up praying for hours for your safety and peace of mind. Don't ever come to me again. I will come to you.

I know now this place isn't for you and I'm glad you're home in your cozy little home with a loving family round about you. Life here is very hard and harsh and only a fool would choose this over any other place on earth.

I've started an ever so small light burning here and it would be cruel for me to leave. It could be extinguished so easily. To the world these lives are unimportant, but to me they mean everything. To start to build and not finish is worse than not to build at all. So, I'll be here for a while, but not forever. I'll build it strong with a good foundation, so it will stand when I'm ready to leave.

I want to thank you for giving of yourself this past week. It's made more precious knowing how difficult the whole thing was for you to do. Settle down now, Bella, and make me happy by being at peace within yourself. Continue loving the family the way only you can do. They will turn around and bless the world and us, too.

I feel a little better after writing. Not so much of an empty feeling inside like it was. Be kind and write as often as you can. I think I'll take a nice hot bath and write a little note to Debbie.

Dear Deb,

Hope you can forgive me for not writing for such a long time. I did write when I said I would, but it ended up in the garbage can. I want you to know I love you just the way you are. Your mom is so proud of you. She had nothing but praise for your stand as a Christian. It made me feel very proud of you, too.

By now, she has probably filled you in on the whole week in great detail, so I won't try to compete with that. For me, personally, it was a wonderful week, and I thank you kids for making it possible.

It's a beautiful morning outside. I got up early and went for a nice long walk in the park before going to work. So, I'm writing this in the club.

Is spring just around the corner? I hope so. Winter is so long and dismal. By the way, I bought a ten-speed bike for twenty pounds yesterday and it was a steal. (Don't take that literally!) so, I look forward to some good riding come summer.

Sorry I sold 'Debbie 2', but with insurance and road taxes so high over here, I felt it was not worth the cost.

When I saw your mom off, I felt a big empty place that lasted a few days. But once I got back working, I felt okay.

Hope this short letter doesn't put you off writing a nice long one back to me, Deb. I do need a lift. I'll sign off for now, but I do promise to answer as soon as I hear from you. Maybe by then, I'll be back to my old writing form again.

Friday Evening, April 30th

My dearest Bella

It's only a few hours since I spoke to you on the phone and the memory of it is still painful. Life can be a tremendous joy one moment and a deep sorrow the next. Change, no matter how painful, is inevitable. How we handle these changes is important. To go on bravely in the face of pain secures us for future joys; to give in to it is to forever live on memories.

For the first time in my life, I am totally incapable of making a decision. I am torn between two worlds. To go home would give me the joy of being with you, Deb, and the boys; trying to make up for your love and faithful support to me. But, in doing that, I kill off a dream that has just been born in the hearts of a few people here; to have a church where their new love for Jesus can find expression in true praise and worship. Where they can invite friends and loved ones with the assurance that our God the Holy Spirit will be faithful to capture their hearts.

With such an abundance of churches all around us, I still must cry out with all honesty, *"We need the real thing!"* Only God knows the answer to our problem, Bella, and I pray that in His infinite love and mercy, He would find pleasure to give me a definite sign to go on in the face of all obstacles, or release me by the end of summer. Either way will bring me joy and pain, but one I can surely live with.

From the Heart of a Husband

So you rest your pretty head, my love
On the breast of God's lovely Son.
At this special time in history
He chose you to be the one
to carry the cup of sacrifice
Like He, in days gone by.

You falter and stumble, but so did He
So never be ashamed to cry
Your humanness and frailty
Are more to be desired
Than the loveliest of sunsets
That dares to be admired

A woman, a mother, a wife, a friend
All come from the richness of you
So rest now, won't you, my lovely girl

Till God makes all things new.
FR

We have a three-day weekend, so I will ask Allen for the use of the mini-bus. I'll rest up tomorrow and take the Northumberland Street kids to the beach Sunday, and the kids from around Lydia's area on Monday. The weather has been brilliant, except for the last couple of days, so I'm hoping the sun will come back.

Tuesday and Thursday Bible studies were excellent, Bella. A young man, Jay, and his girlfriend, Beth, came to the Lord. They are alcoholics, so they have a tough fight ahead. He has come to the Lord a couple of weeks earlier, but did it again in a deeper way after attending a couple more studies.

Fred's mother had some problems she needed help with, so I was invited over for dinner. She must have thought I was a horse; she gave me enough food to feed three people! The sad part is, it was so good, I ate the whole thing!

I want to go on dreaming just a little longer that an ordinary guy like me can be used to change a community for Jesus. I want to feel when it's all over I gave my best, so the future can be free from things I *'should have done.'* So, I ask you to be patient just a little longer. Keep writing and encouraging me, and of course, pray for God's divine wisdom to be mine in these next few months.

Saturday, May 8th

My dearest Bella,

God is very good, indeed. I'm going home for two weeks, and it doesn't cost a dime! I want you to praise Him with me that He won't put on more than we can bear. In my struggle over your loneliness, I received a beautiful letter of love from Debbie that lifted me no end. Then the new convert, Jay, said he was able, through his job, to get me a discount fare if I ever needed it.

I checked with Allen and he gave the okay to take my other two weeks' vacation with pay. The news came back from Jay that my fare would be eighty-nine pounds round trip from Liverpool airport, which my vacation check would more than pay for. Can you believe all that?

Let's not ever get so despondent we lose sight of His loving hand directing every tear. *"They that sow in tears shall reap in joy!"*

Now, I will be bringing a youth with me from the 468 club, but I won't go into any great detail till I get there. The basic outline is this. Greg is not my favorite youth by any means and would be far down the list of my choice for such a dream trip. That's why we must all the more see God's hand in it. Greg is a true 'scally', but is the one who has expressed on many occasions the desire to end it all. I felt the need to give him a dream, something he could look forward to in the future. I promised to take him to America next summer.

Each time he felt down, he would pump me full of questions about our summer trip and I would play it like a game. In his negative attitude he never thought it could happen for him. We both played the game well. When I came with the sudden news I was going, I could see he wanted to grasp for his dream now, as he never fully believed it was for real next year.

I went back to Jay, not really believing I could get the same deal for Greg, but I did! Now I was faced with the reality of taking Greg home with me, which wasn't a pleasant thought at all. I was somewhat relieved when Greg's efforts to get the one hundred pounds failed. He gave up with, *"I knew it wasn't for me."*

Young Billy was dying to take his place and I wanted in my heart for it to be Billy. But, that night alone in my room, I was torn between my desires and the vision of Greg rejected once more. But, I had to think about you and your feelings, Bella, and Billy would be so much more of a delight to have.

By the next morning I was totally confused, so before I went to work, I gave it all to the Lord. *"Father, I want Your will to be done."* And I meant every word. I knew He would show me and it would be right. Soon after I got to work Allen got a phone call saying the Prince Charles Trust Fund would cover Greg's plane fare! We are all happy in the club that Greg is going, but none happier than me! We have set it up as a club project and all have a hand in it.

Greg's dream has, in a way, become their dream to go to America too, through him. This is his moment. Let's give it all we've got, Bella. Don't look at the outside, but what is happening inside.

By the time you get this, I will have talked to you on the phone in detail for time of flight and arrival. See if your mom would be interested in a visit to give Greg a tour of San Francisco. I hope Tony, Frankie and Jimmy will take up the challenge and give Greg a little time.

"All things work together for good to them that love the Lord." And we sure love our Lord, don't we, honey! And I love you too, and hope this will make you happy. That is my one desire.

Note: *Sadly, Greg's dream trip to America never came to fruition. Jay, for some strange reason, had perpetrated a hoax on all of us. He never did work for the airlines and therefore could not get the fantastic deals he'd promised. I figured he'd started out with one lie, him working for the airlines, which led to another lie, etc. When asked about the hundreds of pounds given to him to purchase the tickets, he just hung his head in shame. He was such a pathetic figure, I decided to just let it go with the empty promise that he would eventually pay it all back.*

Saturday, June 12th

My dearest Bella,

It's a week since I left you, and I'm not quite over it yet. I wanted to write as soon as I got back so you wouldn't have to wait so long; but found I couldn't. Hope I can get back into the swing of things pretty soon. Thank you for a wonderful two weeks. I really enjoyed it. I only hope it was worth the sacrifice you and Debbie made to make it possible.

My trip back was uneventful. A smooth flight with a good movie, 'Chariots of Fire'. Got back about five p.m. Saturday and wanted only to go to bed. Instead, I got a quick bath and went on to the praise singing at Lydia's. I was more dead than alive, but the evening was good with a houseful of happy new Christians. It was worth the sacrifice. Sunday I slept in till after one and went to Mark's church in the evening.

Because of the good weather, we've been taking the youth out on trips every day, which was fine by me. The Bible studies have been good. Danny finally gave his heart to the Lord! It was a very moving experience for both of us, as he came to visit me in my room. I didn't make it easy for him, telling him it was going to cost him everything and warning about what he had to face from the youth. He insisted he was ready. After we prayed, he had tears in his eyes and said, *"I feel great now."* He's not kept it a secret and has had many opportunities to share with the youth, who have taken it quite well. I think it came as no surprise to them.

Through him sharing, Billy wants to come to the next Bible study to *'see what this is all about'.*

It's been a long hard week for me physically. I've done battle with the youth over their continued abuse of the youth leader, Allen. I've also had confrontations with a youth worker for putting up anti-government posters in the club.

But more than anything else, I need your prayers for me. It's a spiritual warfare of such intensity, I can cut it with a knife. Satan has these people lock, stock and barrel. I'm no match for it, except if God intervenes in a powerful way. Sometimes I am so weak I can't even pray, so you be that one to fill the gap, Bella.

Hello, my sweet apple blossom,

I'm sitting on my bed just wondering how and what you are doing on this beautiful Sunday afternoon. I have my windows open wide listening to the sounds of life filtering through. Voices of children playing in the street, dogs barking, music from a radio somewhere in the distance and the ever present jingle of the ice cream van that is so much a part of Liverpool.

God has given me such a deep love and appreciation for you and our family, I know it will keep us in perfect peace and harmony, regardless of the tests and trials that are bound to come our way. In true love, absence can only make love stronger; the other belongs to the world and can never be relied upon to hold true, let alone grow. Isn't God good! To take a scoundrel like me and put something good in there.

> *The Lord has guided our last few Bible studies to the very vital area of degree of commitment to Jesus the Person. As young Christians, they are forced to look into themselves with all honesty and reflect on their reasons for coming. To feel good in the meetings will pass away, along with all other reasons I suspect have been cropping up. To draw closer to the One who loved, died and gave us life is the only reason for coming together.*
>
> *If our roots are not grown deep in him, the first wind of change will blow them away. The good feelings will be forgotten and the world will draw you back without realizing it happened. Just another of thousands who tried it because it sounded good, but never got close enough to see the face of Jesus.*
>
> *Turning back is a way of life here, but I blame that on the ones whom God has chosen to preach the Word. It is much easier to tickle the ear than to sting the heart; to be the leader of a happy, contented crowd than the instigator of a broken and contrite heart. Only from the latter will the wind of change blow across this land.*
>
> *Jesus was conqueror only after He laid down His*

life. He said, "Father, is there another way?" Do you think God didn't wrestle with that? Of course He did! It must have been agony to see Jesus suffer that way. What anguish the Father must have felt to have His only and ever obedient Son ask God to search His infinite wisdom for another way to redeem the lost. The Father's heart was broken as He broke the news with tenderness. "No, Son, there is no other way but for you to die."

We, the 'great' stewards of God's word, constantly look for ways to make this Word more pleasing and palatable to a self-centered and pleasure-seeking world. "Surely, Lord, you don't mean dying to self and living wholly for Jesus? I can't get many people to go for a total sellout unless we make it attractive for them. Is there another way?" God's heart is broken again; '"No, children, there is no other way." We, like Jesus, must say, "Not my way, Father, but Your way."

If we are faithful in preaching the truth, God will be faithful to His Word and will save to the utmost all them that believe. If we preach any other gospel, He is under no obligation at all to honor it, and it becomes fruitless to preacher and hearer alike.

Well, my lovely wife,

I am at my limit waiting for a letter from you. It's been over two weeks now and I can hardly stand it.

Work at the club is going fine. More than anything else, that place has brought me into reality of life. I'm learning so much from my experience in dealing with these young lives on a day to day basis. Unemployed, uneducated, unskilled, no motivation, nothing to hope for or look forward to. Mad at the world; mad at society, parents, and anything in authority. I love them, even though they frustrate and make me madder than hell sometimes.

God has made them special to me for His purpose, which hasn't been revealed to me yet. I sense I am special to them, too, and only God knows how grateful and humbled by that I feel.

Got a letter from a youth who joined the Army and I wrote back the same day. Fred's wife will have the baby any day now. Danny still struggles with his marriage, but with him becoming a Christian and faithful in coming to the studies, I think it will all work out in time. Young Billy still hasn't come to a meeting, but I feel he wants to and will someday. Danny shared with him on our day out in Wales last week, so something is on his mind.

Lydia continues to be one of those special people God gets a hold of from time to time. She is tirelessly working for Him and her faith knows no bounds. She has her hands full, too, with a group of girls who have become Christians. Dale, a distant cousin of mine, came to the Lord about a month ago and is doing fine.

Saturday, July 2nd

Hi, Bella,

At my worst possible moment God opened a door to share the Gospel in full with a roomful of the youth. For a whole hour their questions came, and God was faithful to answer them all. It was electrifying as their little worlds came tumbling down. I feel I am on the threshold of a new beginning, and I feel the need to fast and pray.

On the outside, things still remain the same or has gotten worse, but God gave us His Spirit for this very reason; so we may see beyond the flesh. Who would ever know God's greatest triumph came at the world's darkest moment: The Son of God nailed to a tree like a common criminal! Who would have known at that precise moment, the Host of Heaven were singing their praises to the Lamb who was slain for the ungodly. How could we ever doubt. Could mere man ever make up such a story? Only a loving God could devise such beauty in the face of such a tragedy. Only the Holy Spirit could quicken a dead heart to such glory!

Can you go with me once again to the Cross and look upon the face of Jesus, and tell Him our lives are His to use for whatever purpose He chooses, knowing the best came to us at the expense of His total sacrifice. At His death the world trembled and new life, new hope, was given to a dying world. *"This truly was the Son of God!"* Even the very one that drove the nails was born again that very moment. Alleluia!

I'm getting carried away here, sitting in a restaurant, trembling all over. I'd better be careful I don't stand on a table and start preaching!

Got in touch with Full Gospel, but after talking with them, I didn't feel free to go any further. The dinner meeting would cost about five pounds and I wouldn't go without a guest, so that's out. Plus, it sounded like a merry-go-round of meetings here, there and everywhere. I call it *'running after blessings.'* I don't think that's where it's at. If we *are* a blessing we will receive His blessing. I have Him. I don't have to go searching after Him. I do go on, don't I, Bella. Sorry about that.

Well, my love. I do want to hear from you more, but I do want your letters to be filled with peace, joy and victory, as you reach out in a new direction. Would love to hear from Deb and the boys, too, if they can find a few moments from their busy day.

All at the Bible study are growing in the Lord except one couple who decided to drop out for a while. The studies are getting a little deeper, more of a commitment and their seat gets a little hotter. Praise the Lord as I share truth. He will separate the real ones from those who are just playing a game.

Took ten youth on a camp-out last week for two days in the Lake District. It turned out to be the best we ever had, even though it rained both days. The feeling of togetherness was a pure miracle, as we shared our food and shared the washing up, too. Not once did I ever ask for volunteers, they just did it!

At one point, I took them for a drive around the lakes and stopped in the little villages along the way. In one of them, we picked up an American hitch-hiker from San Diego who was a school teacher. The boys were full of questions and we had a fine old time discussing things, when one of them asked if he read the Bible. He said, *"Yes, I carry it with me all the time."* They asked him some things from the Bible and I got the shock of my life. All his answers were the modernist view. Totally void of the power of the Cross and salvation.

I had no choice but to ask for his Bible and proceeded to read all the Scriptures he had so blatantly disregarded. He was left without any defense and the boys were able to see firsthand the true and the false. Danny was made up because, at first, the man had sounded so intelligent.

Got to end now, the restaurant is full! I sometimes sit for hours writing my letters, so feel obligated to give up my table whenever this happens.

Saturday Morning, July 10th

My dearest Bella,

Life is incomplete without you! At the end of my day of joy or sadness you're not there for me to share with. I guess that's why Saturday mornings have become so very special to me; to sit and talk with you.

A lovely Christian couple lost their baby last Sunday. The baby just never woke up. Danny and I went to visit them and came away amazed at their total trust in the Lord for giving them four beautiful months to enjoy that new life. The service Thursday was one to be remembered. I felt proud to have known such a couple, and proud that my Lord was the same one burning in their hearts. The ultimate test of our faith will always be, *"Are we willing to give up that which we hold most precious?"*

The Bible studies are moving into high gear as the Lord deals in ever deeper things. Danny, Lydia, and some of the others want to be baptized next Saturday. They want it to be in a lake with guitars and singing and a family atmosphere. Each will bring some food and make a day of it. They have really caught on to the significance of this occasion; all except one, she was baptized as a baby and feels that's good enough for her.

One of my studies was on the meaning of Jesus saying, *"I wish you were hot or cold."* I could see this didn't go down too well with the above lady, but the others loved it. I have stressed many times that the Lord isn't too impressed with just another group, but is looking for a people who will catch a vision and burn with desire to see souls saved and Toxteth transformed. The cost is great, but the rewards are much greater. I believe the answer is to walk, trust and live in the Spirit. The fruit will come from that.

Life in the club is going fine, Bella. A real change in attitude is evident. If a stranger were to walk in, he would think that statement is a lie, but he would have to have experienced it a year ago to see the difference. Plus, my feelings come from living and working closely with them and knowing what goes on inside of them that is contrary to the outward appearance. Before, there was no battle for good or evil, because evil is all they had known. Now, thanks to God, good is in their midst and so, the battle. I know their struggle and I can see the good is slowly starting to surface through all the junk.

> **Most people will only see the junk, but I can see the tiny nuggets of gold ever so small to the naked eye, and I can sense the youth saying to me, *"Is it worth anything?"* and by my actions I'm saying, *"Yes, it's brilliant, when the sun hits it just right."* At a gold mine, mountains of earth are left behind to remind people that it was worth removing all that for a *handful of precious metal.***

Lake Baptisms

Post Script:

I wish with all my heart, that I could give you, the reader, some sort of dramatic, climatic ending to this story, but I can't. That part wasn't up to me, and God never promised there would be one. It is what it is. If it were a movie or a fiction novel, I'm sure I could have provided a modern version of the parting of the Red Sea with the Mersey River, or churches suddenly filling up with Toxteth 'scallies' exchanging their rags of shame for robes of righteousness. God only asks that we be willing to go into the field and plant and water. He is the only One able to look upon the heart of man and know when it is time for the Harvest.

I know some of my seed fell by the wayside; and the birds came and devoured them. Some fell on stony places, where they did not have much soil; and they immediately sprang up because they had no depth of soil. But when the sun was up they were scorched, and because they had no root they withered away. And some of my seed fell among thorns, and the thorns sprang up and choked them. But others fell on good ground and yielded a crop: some a hundredfold, some sixty, some thirty. (Matthew 13)

I am 73 years of age now. Thirty years have gone by since penning my last Liverpool letter home: a lot of time for reflection. Yes, I'm glad I did it. Even in this late stage of life, I would do it again if the Lord were to call me. But now I would have the maturity. And I wouldn't go anywhere unless I was sure it was His voice calling. I know His voice so much better now. (John 10:4)

Conclusion

In the thirty years since writing the ***Letters from Liverpool,*** our lives have not been without drama. A great loss to us was our youngest son, Jimmy, who died in 1993 due to a drug overdose. He was 27 years old. Bella wrote of those years in a book called, the ***Crystal Hummingbird.*** Later, in another book, ***Pride Kills – Forgiveness Heals,*** she wrote about the six-year impasse my daughter and I had, being estranged from each other; which nearly destroyed our marriage and family.

On the brighter side, at the age of 49, I graduated from college with a four-year degree in youth counseling. I went on to work in youth corrections for the next ten years.

In 2002, while retired in Arizona, I decided to take one last stab at my youth and hiked for eight days through the lush countryside of England following the River Severn. I wrote about my journey in a book called ***I Survived the Severn River Walk.***

Like the song says, *'Through it all, we've learned to trust in Jesus,'* there is no easy path through life. When the going gets really tough, that's as good a time as any to throw yourself into the arms of Jesus and let Him help you work it out.

For the last five years, Bella and I have found a deeper love and appreciation for each other; also a much deeper love for our Lord and Savior, Jesus Christ. Our most special and cherished times together are when we just sit and share what God is saying to each of us through His Word. We truly have that *peace that passes all understanding.*

Photo Credits

Taken by the author in 1981 from the Warwick Street Towers overlooking the tenements in Liverpool 8:

Front Cover: The Protestant Cathedral stands tall in the distance against the leaden sky; while the Catholic Cathedral appears as a crown barely discernible to the right close by.

Back Cover: The majestic twin Liver Buildings (as in a**live**) on the left flank the distant Mersey River and Higson's Brewery towers over the waterfront.

Inside Photos:

#1. Photo of original first and last letters

#2. Las Palmas Grand Tennis Team: Taken by a fan in the Spring of 2011 in Mesa, Arizona.

#3. Rossiter Family: Taken by the pastor who moved us into the once-derelict Falkner Street property in 1974.

#4. Family Collage: Goodbye and God bless as Dad leaves our family in Tumwater, Washington.

#5. Bible Study Group New faith begins.

#6. Frank and his mates from the 468 Club

#7. Toxteth Riots Images from old newspapers.

#8. Caving Adventure The 468 Club leaders and boys, along with the mini-bus are aboard a river transport en-route to exploring caves.

#9. Group Baptism Taken at a secluded lake in the countryside.

Thank you for sticking with me to the end. I welcome reader comments and questions, and look forward to hearing from you at **frankrossiter97@gmail.com**.

Also, if you would like to order signed copies of *Letters from Liverpool*, contact me at the email address above.

About the Author:

Frank J. Rossiter is a retired business owner and the author of *Frankie Boy* and *Letters from Liverpool.* He and his wife, Bella, have been married for 53 years and are enjoying retirement in Mesa, Arizona.

Frank's wife savored and saved every emotionally-charged letter that crossed the continent between them for eighteen months. Were those years for him a mid-life crisis, hoping to make a relevant contribution to the world? ***Or was it a calling from God to fulfill a divine appointment***. Sixty-four letters were saved for over thirty years in her treasure box. Rediscovered, Frank hardly recognized the starry-eyed, romantic, poetic optimist, who wrote prolifically about every aspect of his physical and spiritual journey. Intervening years had rubbed a raw patina of floundering failure he believed worthy of being gone and forgotten...until in God's fine timing, Frank's ***first love for Jesus Christ*** was revived. Like Moses restored after forty years in the desert, Frank is once again ***"drinking from the well that never shall run dry."***

Letters from Liverpool is proudly published by:

Creative Force Press

Guiding Aspiring Authors to Release Their Dream

www.CreativeForcePress.com

Do You Have a Book in You?